2nd Edition

Mega Producer
Results in Commercial Real Estate

By Robert L. Herd

Mega Producer Results in Commercial Real Estate

Robert L. Herd

Executive Editor: Sara Glassmeyer

Project Manager: Elizabeth King, Cenveo Publisher Services

Product Specialist: Deborah Miller

Manager, Creative Services: Brian Brogaard

Cover Image: f11photo/ iStock/GettyImages

© 2018 OnCourse Learning

ALL RIGHTS RESERVED. No part of this work covered by the copyright herein may be reproduced, transmitted, stored, or used in any form or by any means graphic, electronic, or mechanical, including but not limited to photocopying, recording, scanning, digitizing, taping, web distribution, information networks, or information storage and retrieval systems, except as permitted under Section 107 or 108 of the 1976 United States Copyright Act, without the prior written permission of the publisher.

For product information and technology assistance, contact us at
OnCourse Learning and Sales Support, 1-855-733-7239.

For permission to use material from this text or product, please contact
Publishinginfo@oncourselearning.com.

Library of Congress Control Number: 2018943461

ISBN-13: 978-1-62980-203-9

ISBN-10: 1-62980-203-4

OnCourse Learning
20225 Water Tower Blvd
Brookfield, WI 53045
USA

Visit us at **www.oncoursepublishing.com**

Printed in the United States of America
1 2 3 4 5 6 22 21 20 19 18

Mega-Producer Results in Commercial Real Estate

A Blueprint for Success

Second Edition

Robert L. Herd
Associate Broker

Brief Contents

	Prologue	*xi*
	Acknowledgments	*xvi*

Part 1   All about Commercial Real Estate   **1**

1	Getting Started—It's Decision Time	3
2	Why Commercial Instead of Residential Real Estate?	15
3	Train Yourself Thoroughly: Learn! Learn! Learn!	23
4	The Advantages of Specialization	33
5	Joining or Creating a Real Estate Team: Is It for You?	43
6	Client Acquisition Techniques	53
7	Property Valuation Methods and Tax Consequences	63
8	The Annual Business Plan	83
9	The Listing Proposal	101
10	Advertising and Marketing Commercial Real Estate	111
11	Writing the Purchase Contract	119
12	Conducting the Commercial Escrow	129
13	Financing Commercial Real Estate	141
14	Managing Commercial Property	149
15	Commercial Leasing	163
16	Success Patterns of High-Producing Commercial Agents	175
17	Conversations with Three Veteran Commercial Brokers	185

vi *Brief Contents*

Part 2 Commercial Real Estate Investment Types 209

18 Single-Family Homes and Condominiums: A Great Place to Start	211
19 Multifamily Complexes, Large and Small	219
20 Office Buildings	227
21 Retail Shopping Centers	237
22 Self-Storage Facilities	247
23 Single-Tenant NNN-Leased Investments	255
24 Land Brokerage	263
25 Mobile Home Parks	275
26 Industrial Properties	283

Appendix 1: Sample Annual Property Operating Data (APOD)	291
Appendix 2: Sample Letter of Intent (LOI)	293

About the Author	*301*
Chapter Review Questions Answer Key	*303*
Index	*309*

Contents

Prologue	*xi*
Acknowledgments	*xvi*

Part 1 All about Commercial Real Estate	**1**
1 Getting Started—It's Decision Time	**3**
2 Why Commercial Instead of Residential Real Estate?	**15**
3 Train Yourself Thoroughly: Learn! Learn! Learn!	**23**
Role-Play the Listing Appointment	26
Role-Play Writing the Purchase Agreement	26
Role-Play Presenting the Purchase Agreement	27
4 The Advantages of Specialization	**33**
5 Joining or Creating a Real Estate Team: Is It for You?	**43**
The Cause	44
The Results	44
The Next Phase	45
6 Client Acquisition Techniques	**53**
Prospecting	54
Referrals	57
7 Property Valuation Methods and Tax Consequences	**63**
Gross Rent Multiplier Method	66
Capitalization of Net Income Method (Cap Rate)	67
Cash-on-Cash Method	70
Market Data Method	71
Internal Rate of Return Method	72
Tax-Deferred Exchanges	77

viii *Contents*

8 The Annual Business Plan   **83**
Month 1   84
Month 2   86
Month 3   88
Month 4   89
Month 5   90
Month 6   91
Month 7   91
Month 8   92
Month 9   93
Month 10   94
Month 11   95
Month 12   96
9 The Listing Proposal   **101**
Listing Proposal   105
Presentation   107
**10 Advertising and Marketing Commercial Real
Estate**   **111**
Advertising   112
The Internet   114
Marketing   115
11 Writing the Purchase Contract   **119**
12 Conducting the Commercial Escrow   **129**
The Listing Agent or Seller's Representative   130
The Selling Agent or Buyer's Representative   134
13 Financing Commercial Real Estate   **141**
Risk Aversion   142
Debt Coverage Ratio   143
Example of Debt Coverage Ratio   144
Determination of Maximum Loan Amount   144
14 Managing Commercial Property   **149**
State-Defined Responsibilities   152
Specific Duties   153
Establishing Rent Schedules   154
Proper Accounting Records   155

Contents ix

Tenant's Responsibilities	156
Landlord's Responsibilities	157
Assignment versus Sublease	158
Termination of a Lease	159
Evictions and Unlawful Detainer Actions	159
Retaliatory Eviction	160
15 Commercial Leasing	**163**
Antidiscrimination	164
Lease Provisions	165
Names of the Parties	166
Dates	166
Description of the Premises	166
Rent and Late Charge	167
Waterbeds	167
Pets	167
Inspection of the Premises	167
Cleaning and Security Deposits	168
Exculpatory Clause	168
Right of Entry	168
Proper Client Representation	169
Types of Leases	171
16 Success Patterns of High-Producing Commercial Agents	**175**
Bruce Suppes	176
Pete Peterson	177
Harvey Mordka	178
Gary Best, CCIM	179
Maureen Vosburgh	181
Debbie Green	182
17 Conversations with Three Veteran Commercial Brokers	**185**
Bruce Suppes	186
Pete Peterson	190
Paul Lindsey, CCIM	198

x *Contents*

Part 2 Commercial Real Estate Investment Types 209

18 **Single-Family Homes and Condominiums:**
    A Great Place to Start   **211**
    Advantages   212
    Disadvantages   213
19 **Multifamily Complexes, Large and Small**   **219**
20 **Office Buildings**   **227**
21 **Retail Shopping Centers**   **237**
22 **Self-Storage Facilities**   **247**
23 **Single-Tenant NNN-Leased Investments**   **255**
24 **Land Brokerage**   **263**
    Subdivided Lots in Existing Subdivisions   264
    Newly Subdivided Land Being Sold to the Public or
       to Builders   265
    Sale of Large Estate-Type Acreage to Custom-Home
       Builders or Homeowners   268
    Sale of Raw Land to Developers   269
25 **Mobile Home Parks**   **275**
    Ratio of Single-Wide to Double-Wide Units   276
    Location   277
    Amenities   277
    Condition of Park-Owned Units   278
    Common-Area Issues   278
26 **Industrial Properties**   **283**
    Light Industrial Space   284
    Heavy Industrial Space   285
    Pollution   286

Appendix 1: Sample Annual Property Operating
   Data (APOD)   **291**
Appendix 2: Sample Letter of Intent (LOI)   **293**

   About the Author   *301*
   Chapter Review Questions Answer Key   *303*
   Index   *309*

Prologue

"I'm in commercial real estate."

You have probably heard someone say those words with a great deal of pride in their voice at some type of function, especially real estate industry gatherings.

There is a hierarchy in the real estate industry, mostly unspoken, that puts the commercial real estate agent at the "top of the heap," so to speak. The common belief among many, if not most, residential real estate agents is that the commercial agents sell all the big properties and reap all of the huge commissions, and "Gee, they've gotta be so smart to know all that tax and financial stuff."

There is a lot of truth to such impressions, but there are some major differences between residential and commercial real estate brokerage practices that need to be evaluated carefully before one steps into the commercial arena.

If you really learn your craft, as I did back in the early 1970s, and keep current on the commercial market, it can be the source of many interesting and fun transactions and some very large commissions. However, depending on how you choose to enter the commercial arena, it can also be the source of frustration and financial problems, so you have to be very careful how you go about it.

So how does one get started in commercial real estate, and once started, how does one succeed in building a career

xii *Prologue*

that can possibly mean annual sales of $40,000,000 to well over $100,000,000?

This book is a working blueprint for successfully entering or transitioning into commercial real estate, so read on and find out!

New to This Edition

In this edition, every chapter has 10 quiz questions designed to reinforce what you have learned. These are followed by five class discussion topics at the end of each chapter to further enhance your learning.

Chapter 1 has slight enhancements on the topic of the proper time to enter the commercial real estate field and the proper financial backing to do so.

Chapter 2 provides additional information about how to convert assets to the cash needed to see you through the startup period. There are other minor additions and clarifications.

Chapter 3 has expanded information about the dangers of hydrocarbon and other pollutants on commercial property; included is what to look for as well as how to assist your clients in handling a purchase if pollutants are found. There is also an extensive section on the value of role-playing, especially role-playing the listing appointment.

Chapter 4 contains a short but effective way to obtain commercial listings that has been proven to work over and over. Don't miss it!

Chapter 5 is a brand-new chapter that goes deeply into the advantages of joining or creating a commercial real estate team. It is enhanced by a recorded conversation I had with a broker I hired

Prologue xiii

many years ago, who has 10 teams in four different states. This is a must-read!

Chapter 6 has expanded information on how to acquire additional new clients and increase your sales, including how to get referrals from many residential agents.

Chapter 7 provides an expanded explanation of the use and effectiveness of the depreciated replacement cost method of valuation and its accuracy in evaluating a property's value. It also gives information about two commercial databases that list nearly all the commercial properties of every kind available in the entire United States, as well as extensive comparable sales information.

Chapter 8 includes a new section about how to set a monthly budget for prospecting commercial property owners. It also gives a detailed description of how to find the proper person to contact if the property is owned by a corporation or limited liability company.

Chapter 9 incorporates a new caution about always asking the client whose property you are listing if he/she intends to acquire another property when the currently owned one sells, and included is why this is important.

Chapter 10 briefly introduces CoStar, an online national commercial databases that has all the information needed by the commercial broker.

Chapter 11 has additions about risk reduction issues that may occur when presenting purchase contracts and counteroffers and tells how to avoid them.

Chapter 12 explains how to properly conduct an inspection of the inside of the rental units in a large multifamily complex.

xiv *Prologue*

It also tells you what to do when you have an open escrow and one of the sellers passes away or has passed away but is still on title to the property.

Chapter 13 adds a new conversation about how a new commercial agent should go about finding a good lender who actively lends on commercial real estate. It also provides a checklist of what to ask the loan officer when the agent interviews him/her.

Chapter 14 contains an added caution about managing properties with swimming pools.

Chapter 15 has a large addition that deals with the issues and responsibilities that arise in proper client representation in the leasing of property.

Chapter 16 shares operational tips from two highly successful brokers whose interviews have been added to the chapter. One broker has 10 teams in four states, and the other broker is the top office leasing agent in southern Arizona.

Chapter 17 has transcripts of conversations I had with three highly successful brokers.

Chapter 18 has several small operational caveats added, as well as a caution to investors about over-purchasing in peak markets and getting beyond their cash reserves.

Chapter 19 includes some small changes as well as detailed instructions on how to budget for, research, set up, and operate a highly effective mail prospecting campaign of commercial property owners. It also reconfirms a method to get run-down commercial property listings very quickly.

Chapter 20 expands on the different types of leases used in office and other long-term tenancies. In addition, it now discusses dealing with potential recorded covenants, conditions, and restrictions that limit tenant types and activities in a business park.

Chapter 21 includes changes in tenant parking requirements as a result of home-based offices and further details on what a Phase 1, Phase 2, and Phase 3 environmental investigation and report entail. The chapter also briefly touches on the concomitant rise of the Internet and demise of regional malls all over the country.

Chapter 22 now notes the importance of conducting an intense interview with potential resident manager candidates.

Chapter 23 contains a new caution advising owners/users to have a hefty and reasonably liquid financial reserve to use in the event of an extended vacancy and offers a way to maximize the return on that liquid investment.

Chapter 24 has no updates or additions. I do not broker land transactions but instead routinely refer them to a land specialist.

Chapter 25 discusses mobile home parks, an investment type I have never sold, and so there are no additions by me; however, Chapter 17 provides the transcript of an interview I recently had with Pete Peterson, who is considered one of the most knowledgeable owners and brokers of mobile home parks in the country.

Chapter 26 deals with light and heavy industrial properties. It is a new chapter that covers many issues consistent with industrial property, such as the large number of environmental and civic regulations, which you will most certainly be required to know; zoning issues; covenants, conditions, and restrictions recorded in industrial parks that you will need to look into as part of your due diligence; types of construction; and several risk reduction issues you will need to be aware of as an industrial practitioner.

Acknowledgments

I would like to dedicate this book to Clyde Rogers. Although he passed on several years ago, he left a legacy of trust, commitment, caring, and sharing with his clients and fellow commercial brokers that still shines like a beacon for all to aspire to. He was a very special guy.

Clyde's patience in mentoring me and teaching me the right way to conduct myself as a commercial broker is appreciated beyond words and will never be forgotten. Thank you, Clyde!

I also wish to acknowledge the information shared with me by Paul Lindsey, Bruce Suppes, and Pete Peterson. Valuable "street-savvy" information like this is hard to find, and very appreciated by me.

Part 1

All about Commercial Real Estate

1. Getting Started—It's Decision Time

2. Why Commercial Instead of Residential Real Estate?

3. Train Yourself Thoroughly: Learn! Learn! Learn!

4. The Advantages of Specialization

5. Joining or Creating a Real Estate Team: Is It for You?

6. Client Acquisition Techniques

7. Property Valuation Methods and Tax Consequences

8. The Annual Business Plan

9. The Listing Proposal

10. Marketing and Advertising Commercial Real Estate

11. Writing the Purchase Contract

12. Conducting the Commercial Escrow

13. Financing Commercial Real Estate

14. Managing Commercial Property

15. Commercial Leasing

16. Success Patterns of High-Producing Commercial Agents

17. Conversations with Three Veteran Commercial Brokers

Chapter 1

Getting Started— It's Decision Time

4 *Chapter 1*

Commercial real estate is as fast-moving and ever-changing as residential real estate is. That's a fact of life, so if you are going to sell commercial real estate, you owe it to yourself and the clients you represent to do it right—right from the start.

Listing and selling commercial real estate with a high degree of competency and truly representing in a professional manner the clients who rely on you for commercial services takes a lot of time and knowledge; it isn't simply something you can dabble in.

Most of the time, the properties you will deal in will be far more expensive than a residential property with many more issues to consider, and there may be extensive tax and/or legal consequences to your client if you don't complete each transaction exactly the right way. Simply put, the risks are larger and the rewards greater.

> Representing in a professional manner the clients who rely on you for commercial services takes a lot of time and knowledge; it isn't simply something you can dabble in.

Two types of people enter the field of commercial real estate. They are the experienced residential real estate agent and the newly licensed real estate agent.

Experienced residential real estate agents usually start listing and selling commercial real estate because they wish to have more overall knowledge about the other areas of real estate. They also want the ability to better represent their clients in a full-service spectrum of their real estate needs, and, of course, the lure of large, even very large, commission checks is always a factor. Another advantage is that most commercial agents seldom work weekends after getting established.

Newly licensed real estate agents who enter commercial real estate are most often seniors at a university or recent university graduates with a degree in real estate. They are often sought out by the large commercial firms like Coldwell Banker Commercial, CB Richard Ellis, and Marcus & Millichap Commercial Brokerage. Sometimes they start on some type of an apprentice program where they are paid a small salary and assigned to a senior agent for up to two years, although this practice is fading fast.

So, what's the difference between the two types of people? Basically, it is two things: the amount of commercial real estate knowledge they have, and their ability to stay the course financially until they start closing commercial escrows. More on that later in this chapter.

Nearly all the universities that offer degrees in real estate teach a great deal about commercial real estate as a normal part of their curriculum. This gives the college graduate with that kind of degree a real edge in understanding how commercial real estate works as an investment and income-producing tool.

The residential agent seeking that same advantage would do well to start taking the courses available through the National Association of REALTORS® that lead to receipt of the professional designation of Certified Commercial Investment Member (CCIM). I'll talk more about that in Chapter 3.

It is common for experienced as well as new real estate agents who start with a commercial brokerage firm to go as much as a year or more before they actually see any commission checks, although this is changing rapidly as a result of the proliferation of teams. If agents affiliate with that type of firm and are not placed in an apprenticeship program where they draw a small salary while they get up to speed and build a client base, they had better have a working spouse, a sizeable savings account, or another means of

6   *Chapter 1*

paying their bills. We will talk about your hidden assets near the end of this chapter.

Agents who maintain their position as a residential salesperson and start to methodically grow their commercial business have the advantage of maintaining the income they receive through the residential commissions until they start to close commercial transactions, but the complete transition may take considerably longer.

I have counseled many residential agents over the years about how to transition from residential to commercial sales by *time blocking*. What I tell them is to block out 10% of their time in their appointment book or daily scheduler to devote to commercial real estate activities, including education, as necessary. Once they completely fill up that amount of time with productive activities, I tell them to increase the time spent on those activities from 10 to 15% and just keep increasing it incrementally until they are spending as much time on commercial real estate activities as they wish to, which could be a full-time transition and an exit from residential real estate.

Which is the best way for you to enter the field of commercial real estate? Should you engage in residential and commercial real estate brokerage at the same time or go to work for a commercial firm? It is really a personal decision that will be unique to each person who reads this book. Your finances and your current income from and enjoyment of the residential real estate market will certainly be deciding factors. If you are married, spousal support of what you are doing will be a major factor.

The advantages of going with a commercial real estate firm are numerous, including excellent training programs, a really high degree of credibility to your commercial clients, the high probability of working on larger, more expensive properties that generate larger commission checks, and the vast amount of property

Getting Started—It's Decision Time **7**

and client research available to you from the support staff at such firms.

The obvious drawbacks are that it takes longer to research who the contact person is for the larger properties because most are owned by limited liability companies (LLCs), corporations, and other entities. Also, finding a "real person" to add to your prospect list can take hours of research, although the emergence of the online database CoStar as a contact source has changed this considerably.

Because you will be working on very large properties, the "authorized signatory" for a given property, who often has to report to a committee of some sort, is more cautious about starting a relationship with you and probably won't work with you as soon as residential clients will. You should plan on spending hours a day prospecting for many months to build a client base before you earn a dime.

If you are an experienced residential real estate agent with an existing client base and you go to work at a commercial firm, you will be required to give up your residential client base except for your clients' commercial real estate needs, and so you will have to refer them to a residential agent. I know from experience that each residential transaction you have to refer to someone else, especially with an established client, will tear at your heartstrings, so be prepared for it.

> I know from experience that each residential transaction you have to refer to someone else, especially with an established client, will tear at your heartstrings, so be prepared for it.

If you elect to stay at or join a residential firm and build your commercial base from there as you engage in residential brokerage,

8   *Chapter 1*

you will have the advantage of continuing to earn commission checks from your residential activities while you are building a commercial client base. Depending on the policies of the company you work for, you may find that you are referred many commercial clients by the residential agents who are not trained in commercial real estate. This is the case at the company I work for.

Paul Lindsey, the former owner of Coldwell Banker Success Southwest, whom you will meet in Chapter 17 of this book, owned his own commercial real estate firm for over 20 years. He is a Certified Commercial Investment Member (CCIM) and an astute commercial broker. He periodically gives classes to a select group of agents within the company who want to engage in commercial real estate brokerage. If they pass his test, they become some of only a small handful of agents in each of the company's offices who are allowed to do commercial transactions. This approach is often very lucrative for them because they have a built-in referral base of 80 to over 100 agents referring commercial business to them, and they may still engage in residential transactions as well.

The drawbacks to entering commercial real estate in that way are the credibility issue, as stated earlier; the lack of available research resources; and the lack of information about what commercial property inventory is currently available on the market, because the bigger firms do not always readily share this information and there is no commercial real estate multiple listing service (MLS). The emergence of CoStar and its huge database of commercial properties—which includes currently For Sale properties, currently For Lease properties, and recently closed property sales—is changing the landscape somewhat in regard to available inventory.

Let's say you decide that you want to jump right into a full-time career in commercial real estate and you are going to need a nest egg to see you through. Where do you find the money? First, be sure that you are totally dedicated to this venture and that you are willing to do everything it takes to succeed, including working long hours every day and spending countless hours prospecting for new clients.

If you are that dedicated, there are several options available to you to find the money to give you the financial staying power you will most certainly need. Just be sure to sit down and plan a very careful budget first to see how much money you will really need. This should also include looking for ways to trim your expenses as much as you can.

First, carefully analyze your *true* monthly expenses. Include everything, including things you pay for annually or every six months, such as holiday presents and insurance. Then assess what income is available to you each month. This could include a spouse's income, alimony, cash flow from investments you own, dividends, and so forth. Deduct your expenses from your cash flow, and you will have a pretty accurate look at how much cash you will need each month until you cash that first commission check from a commercial transaction. Consider these options:

Savings. There is nothing better than having plenty of cold, hard cash in the bank to draw on while you are in your startup mode. If you are already in real estate sales or have another job that produces cash in excess of your expenses every month, there is nothing wrong with saving for a few extra months until you have a year's worth of savings in the bank before you make the change. You'll sleep better at night!

Retirement plans. While many people have large amounts of money in these plans, the money is not easily drawn out without large penalties, and you are basically robbing your future for your present unless you replace it, and so drawing on this type of asset should be a last resort.

10 *Chapter 1*

Home equity. There are two methods of removing equity from your home: a total refinance of your existing loan, or a new second loan or equity line of credit. If your existing first loan has an unattractive interest rate, you may want to consider refinancing it and pulling out the additional cash you will need to get you through the next year. Be sure to include approximately 10 payments on your new home loan if you can. If your first loan is already very large or has an attractive interest rate, it would probably be wise to leave it alone and get a new second loan or equity line of credit loan.

Borrowing from friends or relatives. As far as I am concerned, this option is off-limits. Although it may seem all right at first, it could be, and often is, a sure way to create bad feelings in the family or to lose a friend. Please just avoid it if you can. If that is the only cash available to you at the time, you are probably not a good candidate to enter commercial real estate full time right now; you should stay put, work hard, and save every dollar you can. While you are doing this, you can still take commercial courses and training as available to help jump-start your commercial career when you do make the switch.

Selling assets. Do you own an expensive car, one with big payments, that you can sell or get out of the lease of? It's wise to do so and buy or lease something less expensive, at least for now. Do you have a recreational vehicle, boat, or camper in your driveway that you seldom use? If you have any equity in those types of things, sell them and bank the cash. Go on; do it! It's your future that you're talking about, and if you do this right, you can buy a bigger, better vehicle later; or, if you are really smart, you could invest in real estate for your retirement.

Review Questions

1. Which of the following preplanning issues should be addressed by a person embarking on a commercial real estate career with a large commercial firm?
   A. sit quietly and write a detailed current income/expense report
   B. thoroughly explore what additional one-time and ongoing operating expenses you will incur when you start your career
   C. create a combined work and personal budget and compare it to your current liquid assets
   D. all of the above

2. You are about to start your commercial real estate career with a large company. You have two months' expenses budgeted for. What should be your next move?
   A. wait, and save more money
   B. see your best friend about a loan to get you started
   C. take a detailed look at any other assets you have that can be converted to cash
   D. both A and C

3. How much of each commission check should you put away in a retirement account?
   A. at least 5%
   B. 3%
   C. 10%
   D. 20%

12   *Chapter 1*

4. An existing client who owns several office buildings calls you and asks you to represent him in the purchase of a self-storage facility, which he knows nothing about. What is the proper way to handle this?
   A. Tell him you will be happy to help him, and start asking agents in your office about self-storage facilities.
   B. Tell him you are not skilled in this type of investment but you will do it if he is okay with it.
   C. Tell him you are not skilled in this type of investment but you will refer him to an agent who specializes in self-storage facilities.
   D. Go immediately onto CoStar, pull up any self-storage units, and send them to your client.

5. Why are young college graduates with real estate degrees sought by large commercial firms?
   A. They are young and will be able to work the long hours required.
   B. They have had excellent training in commercial real estate.
   C. They have a long career ahead of them.
   D. all of the above

Class Discussion Topics

1. John has been engaged in residential real estate brokerage for 10 years and makes approximately $75,000 a year, mostly serving repeat and referral clients. He wants to do away with as much weekend work as he can to spend more time with his family, and he feels that commercial real estate is the answer. What advice would you give him?

2. Raphael has been in commercial real estate for two months now, specializing in multifamily brokerage. His dad called to ask him to sell his motel for him. What do you think is the proper thing for Raphael to do, and why?

Getting Started—It's Decision Time 13

3. Charlene Ming just went to work for a large commercial brokerage company. They have placed her in the retail section, where she is to concentrate her efforts on listing and selling retail shopping centers. What are the three most important things she can do to get her career quickly off the ground?

4. What are some of the personal assets that many people have that can be converted into cash needed to get them through the startup time in commercial real estate? Is there any special order they should use, and if so, why?

5. What is the least desirable way to get cash to see an agent through the startup period, and why is it the least desirable?

Chapter 2

Why Commercial Instead of Residential Real Estate?

16   *Chapter 2*

Soon after I entered the real estate business as a residential agent in 1972, I became intrigued by commercial real estate and how it worked as an investment, tax shelter, and cash-generating vehicle. I was fortunate that the broker I worked for rented a room in his office to a highly experienced commercial real estate agent named Clyde Rogers. I was very young at the time and full of questions, and, fortunately for me, Clyde was fatherly and gave freely of his time and his knowledge.

He shared a wealth of information with me about the various types of commercial real estate. I contacted every place I could think of to get books to read about how to successfully list and sell commercial real estate. While I was busy becoming a mega-producer residential agent, I started building a client base of commercial clients that would turn out to be a virtual, fun-filled gold mine!

Although Clyde passed on several years ago, I think of him often and thank him to this day.

I always enjoyed the "thrill of the chase" of selling residential real estate, and it produced a very high income for me (so did managing a residential office, which is my true love in the real estate business). I have always been intrigued by the art of matching an investor with just the right income property to meet his/her tax shelter, cash-flow, or estate-building needs. It's just plain fun and highly rewarding, financially and otherwise.

Because of how I started and the success I enjoyed, I found it most rewarding to engage in both commercial and residential real estate brokerage at the same time, but I must admit that, looking back over the past 46 years, I often wonder where life would have taken me had I made the switch to a commercial firm back in the 1970s.

When my wife and I made the move to Arizona in 1999, I was asked to join the Phoenix office of one of the largest commercial brokerage firms in the United States, where I specialized in retail shopping centers. It was an interesting and rewarding experience. I must say that the firm's training, which even veteran agents like me must attend, was very thorough and fully prepared me to conduct business at a highly professional level and with great skill.

It was only the love of managing a real estate office that took me away from the Phoenix brokerage when I was offered the position of branch manager of the flagship office of Tucson's oldest real estate firm—a decision I have not regretted.

But what about you? Why should you switch to or enter the world of commercial real estate in place of residential brokerage?

It seems that the most talked-about reasons for working in commercial real estate rather than residential are less weekend work, bigger commissions, and the opportunity to work with people who make decisions based much more on return on investment than emotion, though that's not always true!

Although it is true that you will seldom, if ever, work a Sunday in commercial real estate, you will certainly work many Saturdays, and you had better plan on working at least 10 hours a day during the week for the first year until you get an established and repeat client base. This is especially true if you work for a large commercial firm because the big firms are numbers based and performance oriented and will expect results sooner rather than later.

Many, if not most, residential firms tend to be much more relaxed about performance standards than the commercial firms are and will not watch your performance and daily activities nearly as much as a commercial firm will. It can be uncomfortable, especially if you are not fond of cold calling. The increased scrutiny and higher performance standards will, however, also tend to make you more self-disciplined about your time management and the effectiveness of your activities.

18   *Chapter 2*

Although the vast majority of your work will be conducted during the week, Saturday and even an occasional Sunday are when some individual private investors wish to get together to sign listings, hear listing proposals, and listen to offers on their properties.

If you are working on larger investments, the majority of the people with whom you work are available only during the week, so there is minimal weekend work, except for doing research, cold-calling individual property owners, preparing property brochures and listing proposals, and completing other tasks. Saturday morning from 9 a.m. onward is an exceptionally good time to contact property owners to introduce yourself and follow up any written correspondence you have sent them.

Smaller NNN investments (in which the tenant reimburses the owner for all the property's operating expenses, including taxes, insurance, and maintenance) such as fast-food restaurants (the land and building, not the business), Midas Muffler shops, and investments of that nature are often owned by individuals and not by a formal corporate entity, and so the owners are usually easier to contact.

Although it is true that nearly all residential purchases are based on emotional fulfillment, it is incorrect to think that all commercial purchases are numbers based or purchased only because of a property's return on investment. Pride of ownership does play a part, but just a part, and location is still a major factor.

It is true that the return on investment is the overwhelming deciding factor almost all the time; however, resale value, location, and pride of ownership remain factors in many commercial property purchases. The exception to this is the Real Estate Investment Trusts (REITs), which make nearly all their decisions based on the return on investment. As an example, one of the ugliest and most forlorn retail shopping centers I had any involvement with

Why Commercial Instead of Residential Real Estate? 19

was in Apache Junction, Arizona. I had come to know the acquisitions manager of a Texas-based REIT, and he was very happy with the information I sent him about this center, even though he had never seen it. It was only when the major tenant decided not to renew the lease on 36,000 square feet that he began to take a more personal interest, and in the wrong direction because this was still a very good investment!

When I sent him some digital pictures, he was less than impressed and began to talk exit strategy with me. I knew that the Salvation Army was looking for approximately that much space, and I put them in contact with each other. I thought that I might have lost the sale if they leased the space, but that center was so barren and plain ugly that the REIT decided to go ahead with a sale anyway once the new lease was signed.

Ultimately, you will have to make two major decisions. The first is which type of person or entity you want to work with. What makes you want to get up and go to work every day? Seeing a buyer grow excited about that special home, or hearing an investor tell you, "Yes, this property gives me the return that I want and meets my needs. You've done a great job, and I'd like to buy it"?

> What makes you want to get up and go to work every day?

The second decision is made if you are sincerely interested in pursuing a career in commercial real estate: How are you going to approach it so that you don't go broke before you get yourself to where you are regularly earning sufficient commissions to provide for yourself and prosper?

I purposely left these two questions for last because I would really like you to reread the first two chapters, so that the upside and

20   *Chapter 2*

downside issues of getting into commercial real estate are really clear to you. Commercial real estate involves work, just as residential real estate does. There is less weekend work. Commissions can be much larger but are more elusive, and escrows can tend to cancel far more easily than residential transactions do. You will absolutely need to prospect for hours on end for a long time if you ever want to build a meaningful commercial real estate client base.

If, after considering all these issues, you still want to get into commercial real estate, then it's time to learn what it is all about, so let's get to Chapter 3.

Review Questions

1. What are the advantages of starting with a major commercial real estate firm?
   A. The firm's training program will generate brokerage fee checks for you faster.
   B. You will be able to conduct limited residential activities until you start earning fees for your commercial real estate activities.
   C. Your residential past and present clients will start investing in commercial real estate through you.
   D. The large commercial firms have training and support not available elsewhere, and you will have more credibility with your existing and new clients.

2. What is one of the most interesting, nonmonetary reasons to get into commercial real estate?
   A. You no longer have to deal with homeowners who want to overprice their homes.
   B. You will receive much higher brokerage fees.
   C. The product mix of the various types of real estate investments makes each one unique.
   D. You don't have to prospect as much as in residential real estate.

Why Commercial Instead of Residential Real Estate? 21

3. How much weekend work is involved in commercial real estate?
   A. some, usually with individual owners of smaller properties
   B. none at all
   C. a considerable amount, especially with signatories named in REIT- and LLC-owned properties
   D. only Saturdays, never Sundays

4. If you are truly considering a commercial real estate career, what are the two most critical decisions you will need to make?
   A. how much money you want to earn
   B. whether to affiliate with a commercial firm or work commercial real estate at your existing residential firm
   C. whether to go "narrow and deep" in your knowledge by working only one commercial property type, or to do it all
   D. both B and C answer choices

5. What are the two most important activities you will engage in when you affiliate with a commercial firm?
   A. prospecting
   B. training
   C. keeping in touch with current residential buyers
   D. both A and B answer choices

Class Discussion Topics

1. When you enter commercial real estate, is there value in getting and shadowing a mentor, and if so, why?
2. Aram has decided to stay with his existing residential firm and slowly learn and earn his way to a full-time commercial real estate career. If you were his broker, how would you counsel him, and why? What cautions would you share with him, and why?
3. You are the designated broker at the residential firm where Gerri works. She has been with you for eight years and has no commercial real estate experience. She just brought you a

22 *Chapter 2*

listing agreement she has taken on a neighborhood retail center that has a gas station on one of its pads. What action do you need to take? What questions do you need to ask?

4. You work for a commercial firm specializing in office buildings. Your uncle just asked you to list his small industrial property for sale, and he wants to make a 1031 tax-deferred exchange. How would you advise him?

5. You have a 40-unit multifamily property listed for sale. It has substantial deferred maintenance (both buildings need a roof, it badly needs exterior painting, and the landscaping is shot). It is in an excellent rental area close to everything, has a high occupancy rate despite the condition, and has a high net operating income. Will this property be purchased on its emotional appeal or its numbers?

Chapter 3

Train Yourself Thoroughly: Learn! Learn! Learn!

24 Chapter 3

As mentioned in Chapter 2, early in my career I was extremely fortunate to have had a mentor who taught me a great deal about commercial real estate, but the most important thing he taught me was to never stop learning. This is true for everyone in the entire real estate industry, but it is even more critical in commercial real estate because of the size and complexity of many of the transactions, the responsibilities that you take on as an agent, and the inherent potential risks that are a normal part of every commercial transaction, both for you as a practitioner and for your clients.

You might be asking yourself, "What types of risks is he talking about?" Let me give you an example. In the mid-1990s, I came across a newspaper ad for a retail shopping center that a well-known residential agent was advertising. I called her to ask if she was cooperating with other agents and if she would send me a marketing package (better known as a "setup"). She sent it to me, and I immediately noticed that there was a gas station on the site. There was no mention of any environmental surveys having been conducted, so I called to ask her if she or her seller had completed a Phase 1 Environmental Site Assessment. She didn't have a clue as to what I was talking about. If an unskilled agent had represented the buyer, the buyer would have inherited a shopping center with two leaking gasoline tanks on the premises and may have been involved in an environmental cleanup that would have cost him over $1 million.

> If an unskilled agent had represented the buyer, the buyer would have inherited a shopping center with two leaking gasoline tanks on the premises.

In actuality, if lenders are involved, they will most certainly require anywhere from a Phase 1 to a Phase 3 environmental survey, depending on what they find, before they will make a loan on a property that contains any hydrocarbons on site, because they can be held liable for the cleanup if they take the property back in foreclosure. A Phase 1 environmental report is only a records check with the Environmental Protection Agency (EPA). A Phase 2 check is an on-site inspection, usually by an EPA-approved firm that routinely performs these types of inspections for lenders. A Phase 3 inspection involves the drilling of test borings and a laboratory evaluation of the samples collected. If hydrocarbons are found, the station will be shut down until the leaking tanks and all contaminated soil are removed and disposed of; if the intent is to reopen, new dual-wall tanks must be installed and the property signed off by the EPA.

The point is that a lack of education could have been a disaster for several people and was certainly an embarrassment to a very good residential agent who had decided to work outside her field of expertise. Don't let that happen to you!

Just as a top residential agent would never even think of going on a listing appointment without completing a detailed comparative market analysis, a good commercial agent would never think of representing an owner without knowing exactly what is necessary to promote and protect the client's interests.

Where can one go to get the information necessary to be fully informed on all aspects of the various types of commercial real estate? There are actually many sources; however, the three best are a well-informed mentor, as I had; the courses that lead to the Certified Commercial Investment Member (CCIM) designation from the National Association of REALTORS®; and in-house training from one of the large commercial brokerage firms. Many good books and CDs are also available from your local, state, and national real estate associations as well.

Let me touch briefly on role-playing. You see, you will not only need to educate yourself thoroughly; you will also need to learn

26   *Chapter 3*

to convey your knowledge and information in a clear and easily understandable way so that your client feels comfortable with your guidance and the information you provide. One of the very best ways to accomplish this is to role-play. The best and most comfortable way to accomplish this is to partner with someone in your office (another commercial agent is preferred), set appointments with each other to meet at your office, and role-play the listing appointment and writing and presenting the purchase contract. Role-playing with an experienced agent or mentor is best, but if there is another new or newer commercial agent in your office, ask him/her to role-play with you. No doubt there will be some mildly embarrassing moments, but let them be learning experiences that are better made with another agent who is likely to do the same as you than with an actual client. This is actually a fun way to learn!

Role-Play the Listing Appointment

Each of you will need to complete, or have completed for you, a comparative market analysis of a commercial property to use in your role-playing. The large firms have people who complete marvelous ones for you; in smaller firms, you will need to learn to complete an analysis yourself. This is a great learning experience by itself, but combined with role-playing to polish your communication skills to properly present the analysis, it is pure gold! Take turns being the agent and the client. Laugh at your mistakes, learn from them, and enjoy the process!

Role-Play Writing the Purchase Agreement

Role-playing writing the purchase agreement sounds easy enough, right? In nearly all encounters in which you write a purchase agreement with clients, you will surely have several questions from them. How do you counsel them as to the value of the property so that they make a market value offer? Do they have a property that must be sold to exchange the equity in it for the property they are offering on? If they are from the East Coast, they probably use closing attorneys instead of escrow. You will need to explain the difference, as well as the value of title insurance. Ask an experienced agent or your broker to make a list of potential questions you may face when writing an offer, and take turns role-playing asking and answering them. This is also valuable experience. Notice that I refer to it as the "purchase agreement," not a contract. When you write a purchase agreement, it is only a proposal from a potential purchaser to the current owner of a property, nothing more; and it is not binding on either party until it is signed, without change, or with agreed changes per a counter offer, and the fully executed documents are received by the final party. That is when you have a contract. To sound as professional as you can, always use the proper terms for the paperwork.

Role-Play Presenting the Purchase Agreement

The skills required to present the purchase agreement are very often used in two different ways today. You may be at an appointment with the listing agent, presenting your purchase agreement in person; or you may have scanned your signed proposal, as many agents refer to the agreement, and faxed it to the listing agent, and you are now talking with him/her to promote the proposal's strong points before presenting it to the sellers. Go through your proposal and make a list of the strong points, such as a strong price, which you have justified by giving or sending comparable sales to the listing agent along with the proposal; a short escrow period; or a large down payment. This role-play training will require you and your partner to write a purchase agreement and present it to

28 *Chapter 3*

each other. As the offer is presented to you, be prepared to take notes as to the effectiveness of the other agent's presentation and give an open, honest critique to each other. Constructively identify each other's strong points and suggest areas for improvement. Make or obtain a list of the most often-heard objections, and use them on each other during your role-playing. After you have both done this several times, you will see your confidence soar.

If you decide on a career in commercial real estate and are fortunate enough to find a mentor, do whatever it takes to soak up every word that this wonderful person is willing to share with you—especially war stories, because they tend to put learning in context by giving you not only fact-based knowledge but also "applied knowledge," that is, experiences that actually happened in the real world and with real or potential consequences.

Take your mentor to lunch; shadow him/her if allowed; and ask what books, CDs, or videos you can purchase to learn as much as you possibly can. If your mentor could use a part-time assistant and you have some spare time, think about helping out. You can even do this while you are selling residential real estate for a time.

> A good commercial agent would never think of representing an owner without knowing exactly what is necessary to promote and protect the client's interests.

The CCIM designation is, to me, the working equivalent of having an MBA and going into business management. The courses are not easy by any means, but they are well taught by tenured practitioners who are CCIM designees; so when you are finished with them, you are so far above and beyond the capabilities of the average commercial real estate agent that there is simply no way

Train Yourself Thoroughly: Learn! Learn! Learn! 29

to make a valid comparison. It's much like comparing the skills of a CPA to those of a bookkeeper.

You will crunch numbers for an entire week until you know in your sleep discounted cash-flow analysis and net present value of future income streams. You will learn more about taxation than you ever thought possible, including its effect on the pre- and after-tax returns achieved by any type of investment property and how and when to use a tax-deferred exchange to get your client an interest-free loan from the government.

You will learn every method of property value evaluation, including the market data approach to value and the capitalization of net operating income approach to value (commonly called the "cap rate"), how to determine what the internal rate of return of a property is to a given investor, and when and how to use gross rent multipliers to value a property. Be careful with this one.

Just when you think that you know it all, you will be taught how to conduct a detailed and well-documented site analysis and feasibility study for any kind of investment property.

Remember what it is that we sell as real estate agents: It's not property—the sellers sell property. We sell our time and our knowledge to people who want to buy, sell, or lease real estate. In my opinion, there simply is no better way to fine-tune your engine for maximum performance in producing an income and being able to give top-rated representation to your clients than to get the CCIM designation.

> There simply is no better way to fine-tune your engine for maximum performance in producing an income and being able to give top-rated representation to your clients than to get the CCIM designation.

30 *Chapter 3*

I was so enamored with real estate office management and residential sales that although I became a CCIM candidate in 1987, I never took the fifth course or completed the follow-up work required to get the designation, though I did acquire all the skills. From time to time I still regret not having finished the course; I hope you don't do what I did.

If you go to work for one of the large commercial firms, plan on going through some stringent training. In fact, if you don't have, at the very minimum, a good working knowledge of commercial real estate and in most cases at least a fair amount of transactional experience, the large commercial firms probably won't even hire you, except for an intern job or as an assistant to a tenured agent.

Some of the midsize commercial firms will hire residential agents who seem to "sparkle," although it is common for these firms to be much more involved in commercial property management and leasing than in investment property sales. They always have an investment division, but it is often a minor part of their operation. If you interview with these midsize firms, be sure to ask detailed questions about their training, the scope of the position you are being considered for, the amount of support available to members of the investment division, and what their market share in the investment marketplace has been for the past few years.

Your interests will be best served by affiliating with a commercial firm that feels like a good fit and staying there for a long time while you build a loyal client base and gain credibility in the local marketplace; so take your time and interview thoroughly before deciding which firm to join.

Your credibility will also be greatly enhanced by attaining a great deal of knowledge about and specializing in only one type of commercial real estate investment. You will learn more about this in the next chapter.

Review Questions

1. Representing a commercial client in a transaction when you know little or nothing about the type of property he/she wants is:
   A. putting yourself and your client at potential financial risk
   B. needlessly exposing you and your client to potential litigation
   C. the quickest way to get a bad reputation and possibly be sanctioned by the Department of Real Estate
   D. all of the answer choices

2. If a client asks you to represent her in acquiring a type of property you know little about, what action should you NOT take?
   A. refer her to an experienced agent, in your office if possible
   B. ask an agent in your office who works that type of property to work with you on the transaction and split the commission according to what each of you brings to the transaction
   C. quickly read up on that type of property and help her out
   D. ask your broker or branch manager for direction

3. What is the top reason for educating yourself well about the commercial property you assist clients with?
   A. promote and protect the client's best interest
   B. promote and protect your own best interest
   C. promote and protect the local real estate association's best interest
   D. both B and C answer choices

4. What is considered to provide the most effective form of "experiential" training?
   A. role-playing
   B. commercial real estate books and CDs
   C. classroom lecture
   D. a combination of books, CDs, and classroom lecture

32 *Chapter 3*

5. You are interviewing with small-to-midsize commercial firms that are also involved in property management and rentals. Other than training and mentoring, what is the most important issue you need to explore before making a decision?
   A. how many of the company's assets are focused on the brokerage division
   B. how many agents are in the company's office
   C. whether the company will let you engage in leasing as well as brokerage
   D. whether you will be allowed to invest personally in real estate

Class Discussion Topics

1. Sara just started in real estate, and has signed on with a residential firm, but wants to act as the commercial referral source for all of the residential agents there. What problems do you see on the horizon?
2. Barry is fairly new to commercial real estate, but he has 10 years of residential experience. He has studied a little about self-storage facilities but has never brokered one. A residential agent in the same firm has come to him to say he would like Barry to help him sell his father's self-storage facility. What should Barry do?
3. Kevin and Elena are role-playing taking a listing. What preparation should each of them have made before their meeting, and why?
4. What are the possible training advantages in working for a large brokerage firm?
5. Patty previously worked for one residential firm for six years and then for three different commercial firms over the past seven years. She is frustrated that she is losing clients to other agents. What do you think are the reasons this is happening to her?

Chapter 4

The Advantages of Specialization

34   *Chapter 4*

Once you have affiliated with a commercial firm or decided to stay with your residential real estate firm and make a slow transition to commercial sales, your next step will be to determine whether you will be a jack-of-all-trades commercial agent or will specialize in one type of investment only.

If you go to work at almost any of the large commercial real estate firms, your decision will be made for you. You will be hired to fill a vacancy in one of the specialized areas, such as retail shopping centers, residential income properties, office buildings, self-storage facilities, mobile home parks, hotels, land, or industrial properties.

If you stay at your residential company, you call the shots. But be careful! It is an easy mistake to make to try to be all things to all people, because you won't want to miss out on any possible listings or buyers. However, your interests and those of your clients are best served if you narrow your marketing and sales efforts to only one or two types of commercial investments, preferably only one.

You may be asking yourself, "Hey, wait a minute, this guy is telling me to go 'narrow and deep,' to specialize, when he did it all! Why the difference?" The answer is that I started in a different era than agents who enter the field now, and I had the most wonderful mentor a guy could ever hope to find. I was given detailed knowledge about every type of real estate investment sale he ever experienced. My training with him was exciting but exacting, and it went on for almost two years! Commercial property owners are more savvy today, though they are often so busy with careers and other distractions that they tend to rely more heavily than ever on the deep skill and knowledge of "their agent."

This gives you the opportunity to go narrow and deep in your quest for saturation knowledge about one type of investment product. You will quickly end up with an intimate understanding

The Advantages of Specialization 35

of whatever type of property you have chosen to specialize in, so that when potential sellers interview you and one or two other agents about listing their investment property, you will shine like a new penny and stand a much better chance of getting the listing or securing them as investors.

> If you stay at your residential company, you call the shots. But be careful! It is an easy mistake to make to try to be all things to all people.

Because you will be prospecting and talking to owners of only one particular type of property, you will be in contact with them more often, you will have better, more interesting conversations with them, and they will come to know and respect you much sooner than if you are "shot gunning around" all over the place.

This doesn't mean that you can't sell other investment property; it just means that you will limit your prospecting and listing activities to a particular type of commercial investment.

Back in the 1970s, when I owned my own real estate firm, I specialized in Victorian apartment-house sales in San Francisco. I kept learning until I had a deep knowledge of apartment-house sales *and* knew almost all the special features found in Victorian buildings, such as 30-amp knob-in-tube wiring and lath and plaster walls instead of sheetrock.

I had about 350 owners in my database, and I mailed an informational letter with a return postcard every month. After several months, as they began to know and trust me, they started sending the postcards back to me requesting more information about buying more units, selling their apartment building, or exchanging their building for a bigger one or one in a better location. Had

36   *Chapter 4*

I not decided to specialize as I did, I would never have built the trusting relationships that I did. It made me a lot of money!

It is even easier for owners to contact you these days because of the advent of email and text messaging. Be sure that every marketing piece you have, including property flyers/brochures and business cards, has your email, cell phone number, and, if required, your state license number on it.

When I went to work for a major commercial investment real estate firm in Phoenix in 1999, I was asked to specialize in retail shopping centers. It only took approximately five months before I developed relationships where people were seriously talking about listing their retail centers with me or buying another one through me.

Even though I had been a broker for over 27 years, I still had to go through the firm's training program in California. When I started with the firm, the first thing they did was to give me a digital camera and tell me to take a picture of every retail shopping center in the greater Phoenix metro area and build a comparable sales book—a "comp book," as it is commonly called in the business. There were hundreds of retail centers. But can you guess what happened? I really started to know which retail centers were where, what they had sold for, who the owners were, who the tenants were, what vacancies were where, how to spot a center that was thriving versus one that was struggling, and which ones were well managed or poorly managed. Can you imagine trying to gain all this knowledge for every commercial investment type? It would be impossible. That's why, when I would cold-call a retail center owner somewhere in the United States and he/she would ask me questions about retail centers in the Phoenix metro area or even about his/her property, I had good, solid answers. That's the kind of credibility that gets people to respect you and do business with you.

> That's the kind of credibility that gets people to respect you and do business with you.

I mentioned earlier about building a comp book for the type of property or properties you are specializing in. I found that the best format was to get a thick three-ring binder. Put a bunch of plastic inserts into it so that you can place each comparable sale, or "comp," into a plastic sleeve and can move each around easily. If you are comfortable with technology, the entire comp book can be put on your laptop or iPad and easily updated.

Insert tabs in the binder, with each city typed on a separate tab. Then, as you make up each comp sheet, you can just insert it in the proper section, under the name of the city, in ascending order by sold price. The sheets are very easy to move around that way as you keep adding to your binder.

When I was taking the pictures, I would take them in jpeg format, which numbers them automatically. I had a spiral notebook that I had numbered from 1 to 350. As I took each picture, I would put the address down, if it was available, or the name of the center and the location (e.g., Safeway Center @ NE corner of Scottsdale Blvd & Shea).That way, you don't get the pictures and centers mixed up.

This comp book is a mainstay of credibility for you, especially when you meet face to face with an owner to talk about listing his/her property. You have one or more pictures of each property, the sales price, the cost per square foot, the location, the name of the retail center or apartment complex, how long it was on the market, and the date of the sale. You also have a written comparative market analysis that compares at least three of these to the owner's property as proof of your skill. It is quite impressive and will

38   *Chapter 4*

help you to quickly gain credibility and get more commercial listings and sales.

> This comp book is a mainstay of credibility for you, especially when you meet face to face with an owner to talk about listing his/her property.

I want to mention one other activity that is almost always a way to obtain new listings sooner rather than later. While you are developing the sphere of properties you want to market your skills to and you are out taking pictures of each of the properties, keep your eyes out for similar but run-down properties in the area. Take a picture of each of these and then mail a letter to the owner with a copy of the picture included. Let the owner know that you specialize in helping owners rehabilitate and market such properties and that you will be glad to assist if he/she is interested. This approach works especially well with out-of-state owners and with multifamily properties, but I have had success using this tactic with strip retail, office buildings, and small neighborhood retail centers.

Be prepared to have someone call you out of the blue to vent his/her frustration. Just be patient and consoling, and tell the person that you are eager to help.

Review Questions

1. What phrase is used to describe a deep knowledge of and practice in only one type of commercial real estate?
    A. saturation knowledge
    B. narrow and deep
    C. professional edge
    D. focused knowledge

The Advantages of Specialization 39

2. What is the advantage of saturation knowledge of a certain type of commercial real estate?
   A. higher commissions per sale
   B. potential competitive advantage over another agent when you are one of several agents being interviewed to handle a commercial listing
   C. superior representation of the clients you represent
   D. both B and C answer choices

3. If you are going to go narrow and deep, what are the most important initial things to do and then maintain?
   A. drive the territory and take pictures of each property you will include in your mailings
   B. go online, find your state's secretary of state website, and save it to your desktop
   C. get a list of properties you want in your database, make a file of them, and save the file to your desktop
   D. all of the answer choices

4. You should never go on a listing proposal appointment without doing which of the following?
   A. pull a few comps out of the multiple listing service to take with you because only sold properties matter
   B. thoroughly research the three comps that are the closest in value, area, size, and date of sale, as well as currently available comps, and prepare a professional looking package to give the owners
   C. not bother with sold properties because they're old news, but just research and take along current listings of like properties and be prepared to discuss the competition
   D. ask your favorite title company to prepare a market analysis for you

40 *Chapter 4*

5. How will going narrow and deep result in more business for you?
   A. You will increase your contact with the owners of that particular type of commercial real estate because your prospecting efforts will be more concentrated, and the owners will get comfortable with your professional knowledge sooner.
   B. You will not have to call each of the owners in your sphere as often as you would if you engaged in all facets of commercial real estate.
   C. You will know something about all types of commercial real estate, and your sphere of property owners will be impressed by this.
   D. You will need to study all types of commercial real estate.

Class Discussion Topics

1. Compare the advantages of the "narrow and deep" concept with the advantages of selling various types of commercial real estate.
2. Nikki has been a commercial broker for seven years. She specializes in multifamily-housing brokerage. An associate in the same office who specializes in retail brokerage has asked her to co-list a neighborhood shopping center valued at $7.8 million. What should she do?
3. Your grandfather is one of four partners in a limited liability company that owns a 179-unit multifamily property. He got the other partners to agree to list with you, but you have never sold a multifamily property yet. What should you do?
4. Jerry Choi specializes in retail shopping centers. He has been asked to list a center that has a major food chain market and a gas station on the property. There are 22 other small businesses on site. The market has 11 months left on its 20-year lease,

The Advantages of Specialization   41

and sales have been declining for six straight years. What research will help him help the owners establish the property's value? What questions should he be asking?

5. Moji is calling owners in his database for the fourth month in a row. Mr. and Mrs. Herrera, whom he has talked with on three occasions, have asked him to help them locate a self-storage property in the $4 million to $6 million range to invest in. He specializes in self-storage and knows the state of the current self-storage market, what banks will finance them, what the banks' maximum loan-to-value ratio is, and what is currently for sale. He also has four other people in his database whom he has talked with at length who are thinking of selling and retiring. The Herreras have told Moji that they are also going to be talking to their son's girlfriend, Terri, who deals mostly in residential real estate but says she will be glad to help them. Who has the better chance of getting the sale, Moji or Terri? Who can give them superior service, and why?

Chapter 5

Joining or Creating a Real Estate Team: Is It for You?

There has been a virtual explosion of real estate teams over the past several years. What is the cause of this enormous growth, and what are the results? The answer has several integrated parts.

The Cause

Every real estate transaction now requires a huge amount of paperwork and involves other related issues. The due diligence inspections of the physical property, the title report, or chain of title for those in the East, shepherding the loan through the lender and assisting the buyers with required lender forms and documents, property condition inspections, and verifying repairs—these are only a few elements of what has become an enormous, time-consuming task. The result of this task load developed what is now commonly referred to as "accordion income"; this is because a productive agent would sell several properties one month but then sell nothing for a month or more because the agent's time was almost fully consumed with shepherding each property to a successful closing. As a result, the agent's income would be great one month but nearly zero the next month. This went on continually all year long!

The Results

There is a saying in real estate that "if you don't have an assistant, you are one." This philosophy—namely, that the behind-the-scenes work that must be accomplished could be handled by an assistant, usually at a generous pay scale that is nonetheless far below what a productive agent could earn were that time available to the agent—was the starting point for hiring an assistant. A note

---

In Chapter 17 you will read a full interview I had with Pete Peterson, who I hired as a new agent in early 2003. He personally specializes in mobile home parks and has 10 real estate teams in five states. He has a wealth of information and knowledge on both, and he welcomes your phone calls and emails.

of caution here: If you do hire one or more assistants, it is just good business for them to be licensed in the state where you are doing business. Virtually every state has a law that prevents an unlicensed person from interacting with clients in the conduct of real estate activities. To do so can mean the suspension or forfeiture of the agent's real estate license, as well as the payment of hefty fines, so be very careful to investigate this with your employing broker and the department or bureau of real estate in your state. If you wish to learn more about interviewing, hiring, training, and working effectively with a licensed assistant, consider reading *Become a Mega-Producer Real Estate Agent: Profit from a Licensed Assistant,* available through amazon.com or BarnesandNoble.com.

The Next Phase

Productive agents started hiring assistants at a record pace. Once the assistant was hired, the agent nearly always became far more productive and made more money, often a lot more money. So, agents began to think about how to amplify their incomes by using assistants in other areas of their work. The result was the creation of the real estate team of trained licensees who specialize in only one aspect of the team leader's production and so contribute to the leader's success as well as their own.

In the next sections I explain each of the specialties a modern real estate team may have and show how they earn their salary by increasing the team leader's production to heights that were only a dream several years ago.

The Licensed Assistant

The licensed assistant is responsible for recordkeeping and ordering For Sale and Sold signs to be put up and taken down, often keeps track of agent production, such as listings for sale and listings sold, buyers represented-closed, buyers represented-not

46 Chapter 5

closed, or "transactions fell through" (TFTs). They also order supplies and business cards, which the agents pay for; send memos to the entire staff of upcoming office meetings and training events; and engage in activities and provide anything else the team leader needs from an administrative standpoint. This is usually a salaried position and is normally a Monday through Friday position.

The Inside Sales Associate

The inside sales associate (ISA) works strictly in the office. This associate's position is totally geared to lead generation and prospective-client nurturing. The ISA's daily tasks include cold-calling property owners on behalf of each outside sales associate (OSA), often in a predetermined area of the community where the OSA agent and company operate, and nurturing obtained leads until the proposed client is ready to provide his/her "numbers" for review and list the property. Once the numbers are ready, they are turned over to the OSA. The ISA is usually paid a portion of the commission earned on each transaction that he/she nurtured to a listing taken by the OSA that results in a successful closing and may also have a small salary as well.

The Outside Sales Associate

The OSA works exclusively outside the office showing property to investor clients, taking and servicing listings, and writing and presenting purchase agreements to property owners. For a talented agent who works his/her craft in the proper manner, this is almost always a high-paying position. This person is paid a percentage of each commission he/she generates through each successful closing. This person is paid entirely by commission. The commission split between the brokerage firm and the OSA is nearly always less than the associate would earn if he/she worked alone, without the assistance of the company and the ISA, but the compensating factor is that OSAs are continually given new business opportunities by the company via the ISA leads that are provided to them.

The Escrow Administrator

The escrow administrator's entire job is to assist the OSA and the team leader with each escrow they open. The administrator's job includes opening the escrow or making contact with the closing attorney, seeing that the buyer's earnest money check is tendered to the escrow agent or closing attorney in a manner prescribed by your state's law, scheduling inspections for the OSA, receiving faxes or email with attached inspection reports and/or seller property financials, accepting title reports and sending them to the OSA for review, sending the OSA reminders of escrow closing appointments and inspection dates, and fulfilling any other requests made by the OSA or the company. This position is also usually a salaried position on weekdays only and may include a bonus tied to the number of successful closings.

Though it is tempting to try to negotiate with your broker to let you use the broker's staff for some of this support, you will lose a great deal of control of and focus on your team's business if you do that; therefore, avoid doing so if at all possible.

So you're an experienced broker who is interested in creating a team. Here are several things for you to consider. First, if the company you are with allows real estate teams, which nearly every company now does, you are almost always better off staying with the company and creating one or more teams than you are opening your own company. Put your ego aside, for there is already much in place that you can take advantage of, usually at a far-reduced cost. When you compare the cost of opening your own company today—rent, technology, errors and omissions and personal property insurance, and supplies only start the list—and weigh the advantages of building a team where you are, nearly all those expenses have already been paid for by the company. So tuck your ego in your back pocket and create the best real estate team in town!

48   Chapter 5

Getting started building your own team involves a step-by-step process that you need to go through slowly and carefully. Consider well whether you are fully ready, both emotionally and financially, for each step.

Step 1 is when you have become so individually productive that you have the "70-hour syndrome." That is when you become aware that you are working 70+ hours per week just to keep up with everything that must be done to show property, write and present offers and counteroffers, open escrows, deliver checks to escrow, order and attend inspections, go over the title report, negotiate repairs, and be at the closing. You suddenly realize that you need to hire your first team member, a licensed escrow administrator. If you hire carefully, after an extensive interview and a thorough reference check, in a few weeks you will suddenly find your time is noticeably freer, and you are becoming more productive and have more time with your family and loved ones.

Your production begins to climb, and you think about what it would mean to you to have someone in the office who does nothing but generate new business for you, and so to hire the next team member, you follow the same routine you used before: You interview carefully, check references thoroughly, and this time hire an ISA. Make sure this associate is licensed, thoroughly trained to use written dialogues in his/her prospecting activities, and fully up to speed on the nature of commercial real estate enough to be credible with the public, and you can then turn this person loose on the world.

The results of a well-trained, motivated ISA will pay big rewards very soon, generating more appointments than you can possibly keep up with. The next step is to hire your first OSA (keep building, and there will be more): Hire carefully, train thoroughly, and set realistically high production goals and enforce them.

Joining or Creating a Real Estate Team: Is It for You? **49**

By this time, and sometimes even before this stage, you and your team will be generating so much business that your escrow administrator will become stressed by the huge increase in the workload. Watch for this, and when you see the signs of stress, hire an additional escrow administrator. Have your existing escrow administrator sit in on your interviews, and ask for and value this person's opinion of each candidate. Never hire someone at the interview, though. Always first thoroughly check out the interviewee, and then call to ask for a second interview. Ask a few stress-inducing questions to see how the interviewee handles them.

Keep in mind that at the time you hire your first team member, you have become a boss and manager. Managing people is a completely different skill set than selling real estate. The National Association of REALTORS® offers CCIM Institute classes to help you become a superb salesperson and CRB (Certified Residential Brokerage Manager) classes to teach you how to be an excellent manager. So if you find yourself lacking in either area, remember that very effective help is only a click of the mouse away.

Review Questions

1. Which of the following is the major cause of the proliferation of real estate teams?
   A. Internet
   B. new real estate laws
   C. huge increase in paperwork and activities required to complete a real estate transaction
   D. increase in disclosures required to complete each transaction

50   *Chapter 5*

2. What is an agent with the 70-hour syndrome experiencing?
   A. exhaustion, heading toward total burnout
   B. frustration with having to be at property inspections instead of showing property or taking a listing
   C. probable loss of income from having to take care of so many unproductive escrow-related issues
   D. all of the answer choices

3. Hiring a licensed assistant nearly always causes which of the following to occur?
   A. The agent's income rises.
   B. The agent's free time increases.
   C. The agent has more productive work time.
   D. all of the answer choices

4. Which of the following statements is true?
   A. A team leader should use the broker's support staff for team business as much as possible.
   B. A team leader should slowly and carefully hire his/her own staff to support team business.
   C. A team leader should hire an escrow administrator, ISA, OSA, and assistant as soon as possible.
   D. If the company broker offers the use of his/her staff, the team leader should take full advantage of the staff for the first year.

5. Which of the following is a very important aspect of hiring team members?
   A. hiring slowly and carefully with much thought as to whether you are ready emotionally and financially for each new step
   B. hiring fast and training fast (If they don't work out, replace them.)
   C. letting the broker know you are moving your team off site and he/she will need to get you furniture
   D. asking the broker's escrow administrator if he/she would like to work for you

Joining or Creating a Real Estate Team: Is It for You? 51

Class Discussion Topics

1. Discuss the pros and cons of forming a real estate team instead of opening your own company. What are the advantages? What are the disadvantages?
2. In as much detail as possible, describe the process of forming your own real estate team. When and how should you do it? How soon will you implement each phase? Why should you do it? What are your expectations?
3. Discuss what you will expect of your OSA. How will you train him/her? What will your minimum standard of production be, and how will you measure it? How will you hold him/her accountable for meeting and exceeding your minimum standard?
4. Once you hire your first team member, you have a new role: You have become a boss. What will you do to see that you, as the team's leader, create a fun, productive environment in which your team will thrive?
5. If you have no experience being a boss and team leader, discuss the various places where you might obtain management experience and training.

Chapter 6

Client Acquisition Techniques

54   Chapter 6

Prospecting

Prospecting has to reign supreme when it comes to creating a database of commercial property owners who will do business with you. Several forms of prospecting are effective.

Cold-calling is an excellent form of prospecting. I know, I know, you *hate* cold-calling! When it came time to cold-call residential homeowners, so did I, and it took a lot of discipline to do it regularly back in the 1970s. (I haven't made any residential property cold-calls since then.) If you have read my second book, *How to Become a Mega-Producer Real Estate Agent in Five Years*, then you read the four interviews that I conducted with mega-producer agents who consistently sell from $40 million to over $120 million worth of real estate each year. None of them has ever cold-called.

Now you're thinking, "Well, if they don't do it, why should I?"

The answer lies in what your competition in the commercial arena is doing, and they are doing plenty of cold-calling! You see, cold-calling commercial property owners is, for the most part, quite different from cold-calling homeowners. You have very little to offer a homeowner when you call (after checking the national Do Not Call list, of course). With all the information available on the Internet, many if not most homeowners have at least a general idea of what their home is worth. What else can you share with them except for neighborhood activities and such?

> You see, cold-calling commercial property owners is, for the most part, quite different from cold-calling homeowners.

But you have much to share with commercial property owners. A large percentage of them do not even live in the state where the property you are calling them about is located. They are almost always receptive to receiving up-to-date information about what is going on in the commercial arena that will affect their investment holdings. Commercial business owners are also exempt from the Do Not Call list.

> Commercial business owners are also exempt from the Do Not Call list.

If you really want to make your cold-calling experiences the most profitable that they can be, take the time to write each investor an introductory letter first. Tell the investors that you specialize in whatever their commercial holdings are and that as a way to get to know them, you will be sending them a complimentary newsletter on a regular basis. Tell them that you would like to hear about what topics regarding commercial real estate would interest them the most and that you will call them in a few days to quickly touch base with them to see what interests them. Always follow up after the call with a handwritten thank-you note because doing so will really set you above the rest of the cold callers who will contact them. I have met some commercial property owners after calling them for three years, and they have kept and proudly show me all the thank-you notes I have sent them.

Look for real estate articles in the local papers, online, and in any trade magazines you subscribe to. Compile them each month and write your own letter, referencing the articles, mailing your database a copy of one or more articles, or reprinting them with permission. If you are a REALTOR®, then you get *REALTOR®* magazine each month; it has a commercial section in it with excellent articles.

Your first call should be to introduce yourself, to see if the property owners received your letter and whatever article you sent along

56 *Chapter 6*

with it, to learn how they feel about the property they own now, and to ask if you may continue to send them local and national information about commercial real estate and especially information about the type of commercial property they own now or would like to own.

With their approval, you should start sending them something monthly for six months, and then every two months. Then follow up to confirm that they received what you sent them, see what their opinion of it is, and find out what else they would like to know. It is much easier than you think!

Make a regular work habit of driving by all the investment properties you have in your database; do this every three months. Note if you see a vacancy sign or a building getting run-down or in need of a roof or some other obvious repair. Take a digital picture of the premises and email it to the owners; when you talk to the owners, tell them what you have seen.

> Make a regular work habit of driving by all the investment properties you have in your database; do this every three months.

If another property in close proximity to theirs comes up for sale, get information about it and send it to the property owners and to others in your database who have similar properties or who have told you they are looking for a property similar to that.

Call to ask the property owners if they have received the information and have any interest in acquiring the property through a purchase or an exchange of their existing investment. Anyone who is interested will want the latest income/expense details, so call the listing agent to ask for them ahead of your mailing and follow-up phone calls.

Once you have amassed a database of properties of various sizes and locations, if an investor tells you that he/she is looking for a new investment of a certain size, a certain location, or a certain return on investment, all you have to do is go through your database to see if anyone there has a property that reasonably matches what is wanted. If someone does, then call to tell the property owner or owners you have a client looking for an investment that seems to be a reasonable match for their property and ask whether they would consider selling their property or exchanging it for something else, given that you may have a buyer for it. This approach can create a significant amount of business.

Have I made my case for how easy it is to cold-call commercial property owners yet? I hope so, because if you don't do it, you are in for a disappointing tenure as a commercial agent.

Referrals

Referrals from other agents are another form of prospecting that is highly effective. Most residential agents do not have the knowledge to handle commercial property sales. They are often not even allowed to handle them because of their company's policies and procedures. If they are a REALTOR® who must subscribe to the Code of Ethics, they must give a potential client written notice that they are unskilled in that type of property sales if that is indeed so.

Obtaining a list of the top 100 or 200 residential agents in your market is easy to do and also can reap you big rewards in referrals of commercial listings and investors if you are consistent in your contact with these residential agents. If you do not belong

58   *Chapter 6*

to the local multiple listing service (MLS), befriend a REALTOR®
who has access to the MLS and ask him/her to print you out a list
of the top 100 to 200 agents in the MLS, including their names,
phone numbers, and email addresses. Be sure to keep good notes
about who does and does not refer to you, and be sure to recipro-
cate with residential leads as often as you can.

Getting a relationship started with these agents is similar to what
you would do with your investor database, except that you will
write an initial letter explaining what you have in mind, which is a
mutual referral agreement that you will help each other build
your businesses to new heights by referring business to each other.
After that, you can keep in touch by sending a tasteful postcard or
even email. I highly recommend that each time you get a referral
from someone, you immediately send that person a handwritten
thank-you note. A word of caution here: You may pay the referral
fee only to the agent's employing broker, not directly to the referring agent; otherwise, you are in violation of state law. Also check
with your broker about giving any type of gratuity to the referring
agent, because doing so may also be a violation of law in your state.

> Obtaining a list of the top 100 or 200 residential agents in
> your market is easy to do and also can reap you big rewards
> in referrals of commercial listings and investors.

If you have built up a fairly strong residential following and are
now at a company where you can no longer service the needs
of these clients, you are a prime candidate to reap big rewards
from this type of referral relationship. Just be sure to make it quite
clear that to continue the relationship, you will expect referrals in
return. Be sure to pick your referral sources carefully because you
will want your loyal residential customers to be happy with whomever you refer them to. It should be clearly understood by your

Client Acquisition Techniques 59

referral recipients that all commercial brokerage with your referral clients will continue to be transacted only through you. After a few months you will find that only a small percentage of the residential agents in your database will be the primary source of your referrals. When I found this out, I reduced that database to only a fraction of what I started with, and I was not disappointed.

Review Questions

1. Why are referrals from residential agents the most highly effective method of obtaining commercial property referrals?
   A. You are presold to the commercial client as a knowledgeable professional.
   B. The referred client is highly motivated.
   C. The referred client is pre-approved for financing.
   D. The referred client knows exactly what to invest in and where.

2. What is the second most effective method of acquiring new clients?
   A. cold-calling commercial property owners
   B. writing a letter to commercial property owners
   C. writing a letter and following it up with a phone call
   D. none of the answer choices

3. What is the difference between residential cold-calling and commercial cold-calling?
   A. Commercial property owners often live far from their property and welcome information about its condition.
   B. Commercial property owners appreciate information about the direction of the neighborhood where their property is located.
   C. Commercial property owners are nearly always ready to sell or exchange their property for a bigger or better one.
   D. both A and B answer choices

60   *Chapter 6*

4. You just hung up the telephone after a productive call to a commercial property owner who is in your database. He has asked you to send him information on his property, as well as recent sales of similar properties in the area because he wants to purchase another investment property in your area. What should you send him?

    A. a handwritten thank-you note, followed up by the information he asked for

    B. the current listings of the type of property he wants to invest in

    C. the past six months' sold properties

    D. both B and C answer choices

5. Someone in your database has called to say that he and his wife are looking for a strip center to purchase. He says they want at least seven units in a decent area with a high traffic count. You search your database and come up with two properties that are a very close match. What should you do before you call the clients back?

    A. send the clients information about both properties and call three days later

    B. find out if the owners of the two similar properties are interested in selling or exchanging, and call your clients to let them know the results

    C. find out if the owners of the two similar properties are interested in selling or exchanging, check the MLS if available, check CoStar for similar properties for sale and current properties sold, and send the clients that information, with a follow-up call

    D. call the clients back and pull up CoStar to check for property while you have them on the telephone

Client Acquisition Techniques 61

Class Discussion Topics

1. Jeremy Aguilar is cold-calling a multifamily database he has developed. He has a client from another state who wants a 60- to 80-unit multifamily property in a certain zip code. What action should he take?

2. Jason Chang sent out introductory letters and a résumé to his industrial property database, and he is following up with cold-calls, sometimes called "warm-calls." Mr. Gillette just told him that if he can find him a 40,000- to 50,000-square-foot warehouse with at least four dock-high loading ramps, at least 400-amp, three-phase electrical service, and a glue-lam roof structure to avoid interior pillars, he will let him list his 27,000-square-foot, 60-year-old industrial space. Jason has been specializing in industrial sales for only a year, whereas Geoffrey is a highly experienced industrial broker in his office. How should Jason handle Mr. Gillette?

3. How long into your career as a commercial agent should you continue to prospect for new business, and why?

4. Bill Davis, a high-producing residential agent, gave Ted Elias a commercial referral and agreed to a 25% referral fee. The referred client wants a NNN-leased fast-food restaurant with at least an 8% cap rate. It has taken Ted 13 months to find the right property, and he feels he shouldn't pay the full 25% referral fee. What action should Ted take? What is Bill's reaction likely to be?

5. Betty Jones specializes in retail shopping centers. She was cold-calling, and a person she talked to said that she and her husband weren't in the market but that her husband had a friend at work who was looking for a neighborhood center in the Brookhaven area where Betty does a lot of business. What action should Betty take, and why?

Chapter 7

Property Valuation Methods and Tax Consequences

64 *Chapter 7*

Income properties are evaluated by real estate professionals and appraised by appraisers according to the amount of gross operating income (GOI) or net operating income (NOI) they produce, as well as other factors such as location, condition, amenities, and strength or weakness of the real estate investment marketplace at the time of the appraisal. These factors can vary greatly, and one particular method of valuation is most often more accurate than another, depending on the type and size of the investment property you are analyzing.

There is one constant in analyzing any property's value that you must strictly adhere to as a real estate professional: You must conduct a thorough rental survey of similar properties prior to your analysis so that you have current rent levels as of the date of your analysis. This will allow you to see if the property you are evaluating has rental rates that are above market, at market, or under market. Anything short of that is an incomplete analysis and may subject your client to a huge monetary loss and you to potential litigation, so make it one of your professional standards to always conduct a thorough rental survey prior to any analysis.

> Make it one of your professional standards to always conduct a thorough rental survey prior to any analysis.

In addition, if you are involved in commercial real estate, you should seriously consider subscribing to CoStar and/or LoopNet. These are commercial real estate databases that an agent can access for a monthly fee; they contain a significant amount of data about all types of commercial properties in any given metropolitan area, including property types; site addresses; whether owned by a limited liability corporation (LLC), corporation, trust, or other entity; comparable sales data; and much more. LoopNet has been purchased by CoStar and will be going away soon.

Property Valuation Methods and Tax Consequences **65**

The methods of valuation are gross rent multiplier (GRM), capitalization of net operating income (cap rate), market data method, and internal rate of return (IRR).

No matter which method is used, an appraiser and you should always double-check the results of the income method of evaluation by checking the comparable sales (i.e., comps) you are using to arrive at a weighted cost per square foot. By "weighted," I mean that you will not necessarily find the average, given that one or more of the comps you are using may be much closer in detail to the property you are evaluating than the other two; this means it will require fewer adjustments in value because of a closer location, similar amenities, and/or nearly the same condition as your subject property. You would give more weight to this comp than to one that you had to make several adjustments to. Once you have what you feel is the proper cost per square foot, you multiply the square footage of each comp and your subject property and then multiply each by the weighted cost per square foot. This should coincide closely with your income method analysis. Some agents use the cost-per-unit method to find the value of multifamily properties; however, this must be used carefully, if at all. The reason for extra care is that you need to be sure the properties being analyzed have a very similar unit mix. Let's say you are evaluating a 30-unit multifamily property with 15 one-bedroom units and 15 two-bedroom units, and your analysis shows an average cost per unit of $50,000. The comps you are using all have 30 units as well, but they are all one-bedroom units. Is your subject property worth more than the others? Given similar condition, location, and amenities, it certainly is! The 15 two-bedroom units will generate more income than the all-one-bedroom units of the comps, and using the cost-per-unit method without analyzing the unit mix would undervalue the subject of your analysis.

Now that we know what they are, let's look at each method and see when they are commonly used.

Gross Rent Multiplier Method

The GRM method is most commonly used with small residential income properties, usually with anywhere from two to 15 or 20 units. This method, though widely used, is often the least accurate of all the valuation methods. The reason is that it simply looks at other recent local sales, takes their selling price, and divides it by the stated gross rents to arrive at a "times gross" factor. That factor is then multiplied by the subject property's gross rents to determine the value. It does not take location, amenities, condition (i.e., the existence or absence of deferred maintenance), lot size, date of sale, current rent levels, or vacancies into account. Because any one of these issues can affect the subject property's value, to ignore them is to inaccurately assess the subject property's value in many if not most cases. This method is still widely used in valuing small apartment buildings because cap rates are very often all over the board. However, be sure to take the other factors into consideration before making a value judgment.

For example, you are analyzing the value of a 10-unit apartment building. Its scheduled rents are $500 per unit per month, or $60,000 per year. Other buildings in the area have been selling for nine times their gross annual rent, so you value this building at $540,000 (9 × $60,000 = $540,000). It sounds good, but what if the market rents of the property you are evaluating, based on your newly conducted rental survey, show that the units could be rented at $600 per unit per month? Using the same GRM, the building is now worth $648,000 ($600 × 10 = $6,000/month, or $72,000/year gross rents × 9 = $648,000), and you would have undersold it for your client by $108,000. Is this a malpractice issue?

Another example would be if you were analyzing two identical buildings that were side by side. One building, which was in good shape and completely rented, sold for 10 times gross income a month ago. The building next door is poorly managed and has a 20% vacancy rate.

Are they worth the same amount of money? Of course not, and strict adherence to the GRM method without considering all issues would give you an incorrect valuation of the property.

Any time you use the GRM as an indicator of value, you *must* look at all the issues described here to see if adjustments need to be made that will affect the value of the property.

Capitalization of Net Income Method (Cap Rate)

NOTE: A property's cap rate defines the investor's return on the property on the day of the analysis only and assumes a cash purchase. To include financing, you must do a cash-on-cash analysis.

We can't talk about cap rates without revisiting something we learned in real estate school when we first became licensed. Do you remember IRV?

IRV is an acronym, usually placed in a triangle (see the example):

I = income (net operating income)
R = rate of return (as expressed as a percentage)
V = value

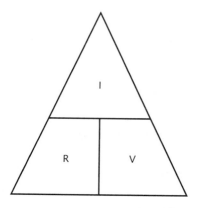

68   *Chapter 7*

To find a property's income, you multiply the value by the desired rate of return.

NOI income example: Value = $1,000,000 × 8% (0.08) or $80,000.
                       (This is net operating income, or NOI.)

To find a property's rate of return (cap rate), you divide the NOI by the value.

Example: Rate of Return = $80,000/$1,000,000 or 0.08 (8%).

To find a property's value, you divide the property's income by the desired rate of return.

Example: Value = $80,000/8% (0.08) or $1,000,000.

This method gives you a more accurate snapshot of the property's value as of a given day or date in time and essentially tells you what your return on your investment would be if you had paid cash for the property on that day. It should still be preceded by a current rental survey, but it is arrived at by taking the gross scheduled income (GSI)—rents and other income such as parking and laundry—and deducting for vacancy and bad debt allowances to arrive at the gross operating income (GOI), then deducting the operating expenses to arrive at the NOI.

The next step is to assess the risks taken by owning the property and determine what return on your investment you would require by taking the risk of owning the property into consideration. If other buildings in the area have been selling at a cap rate of 8% (NOI ÷ Sales Price = 8%) and if your rental survey shows that this building could achieve or is achieving an NOI of $80,000, you would divide $100,000 by 8% ($100,000/0.08 = $1,000,000 value), as shown.

Is this method completely accurate? Although it is usually much more accurate than the GRM, you still have some work to do.

What if the current NOI is only $80,000, but your rental survey finds good demand in the area, and your client could increase the net rental income to $100,000 within six months? Should he/she pay $1,250,000 for the property and still take on the burdensome chore of increasing the rents and face the vacancies that may arise by increasing the rents? Probably not; instead, you would value the property somewhere below the maximum value that *could* be achieved because of the risk assumed by the new owner and the loss of scheduled rents that he/she would realize until they did increase the rents.

You would use an Annual Property Operating Data (APOD) sheet to perform an analysis of this type. The APOD also allows for the deduction of *debt service* (i.e., loan payments) to arrive at pretax cash flow. An APOD sheet has been supplied for you in Appendix 1 of this book. The APOD details the following information:

- *The top portion* allows you to write the date the form is filled out; the property's list price or any other price being analyzed; existing and new or proposed financing; the purpose of the APOD (for analysis purposes, write "Broker's Reconstructed Statement"); the name of the property, if any; the address or location of the property; and assessed or appraised values.

- *Gross scheduled rental income* is the amount of rent that could be obtained if the property were 100% full all the time. (Remember your rental survey!)

- *Other income* is for coin-operated-laundry income, garage rentals, and any other income-producing activities on the premises.

- *Vacancy and credit losses* allow for the real world where vacancies occur and people skip out on rent. A multifamily property is almost never 100% occupied all year long, and most

70   *Chapter 7*

commercial brokers use a 5% vacancy factor +/– for condition, etc., if the owner's records are unclear.

- *Gross operating income* is the real-world income the property is currently bringing in or the amount it would bring in on a pro forma basis per your rental survey.

- *Operating expenses* detail the actual costs to operate the property. Be very careful to see that these are accurate and reasonable. This sometimes entails calling utility companies, property management firms, and other product or service suppliers to obtain or verify information about the actual cost of a particular item or service. Try to estimate the new property taxes when filling out an APOD because doing so will provide your client with a more accurate net income figure.

- *Net operating income* is the amount left over after all income is collected and all operating expenses are paid. This is the figure used to calculate a cap rate and is the amount left over to pay for any debt servicing (i.e., loans) on the property.

- *Debt service* is the amount of money necessary to pay any loans and is deducted from the NOI.

- *Cash flow before taxes* is any remaining money after all operating expenses and debt servicing are paid. This is the figure that is used to calculate the "cash-on-cash" return for the property being analyzed.

Cash-on-Cash Method

The cash-on-cash value of a property is determined by dividing the pretax cash flow by the down payment and nonrecurring acquisition costs or total equity in the property. If a property is financed, or will be, the interest rate of the existing or new financing will have an effect on the cash-on-cash return of the property. The higher the interest rate, the lower the return because more of the NOI is used for interest payments in the debt servicing. If you are representing purchasers of an income property they are financing, it is always good business practice to perform a cash-on-cash analysis for them because it gives a more accurate picture of the true return on the total amount of money they have invested in the property.

Market Data Method

The market data method is always used in evaluating owner-occupied, single-family homes and condominiums. It is often used to evaluate rental property if there have been several similar types of property sales in the immediate area, and it is always used in conjunction with either the cap rate or the cost-per-square-foot approach if the property being analyzed produces an income stream. It is always used to evaluate land and other types of non-income-producing real estate such as a church or school. When analyzing the value of non-income-producing improved property, the market data method is used in conjunction with the depreciated replacement-cost method as well.

Using this approach, you arrive at the value of a property by comparing it with other similar properties that have sold recently, usually within the past three months if possible, and as close in proximity and size to the subject property as possible.

Although a rental survey is not conducted if there is no income being produced, the evaluation process still requires making comparisons of the comps and then making adjustments to value based on such factors as date of sale; utility and zoning; availability of utilities, as in the case of land; condition, overall utility, and size of the structure(s) included in the sale; and the strength or weakness of the market.

A good example of why this is important is illustrated by a land sale that was being negotiated by one of my commercial guys as

72   *Chapter 7*

this book was being written. He wrote an offer on 126 acres of land in southern Arizona for $2.1 million. During the feasibility study period, he found that nearly 30 acres are either in a flood zone and thus not buildable or abut a Native American reservation and have restricted use. Needless to say, the price was renegotiated.

Analyses of commercial properties requiring use of the market data method of analysis and/or the depreciated replacement-cost method are often undertaken by a certified appraiser with a Member of the Appraiser's Institute (MAI) designation, or equivalent, and the analysis often costs several thousand dollars.

Internal Rate of Return Method

The IRR method of valuation is most commonly used by institutional investors such as real estate investment trusts (REITs), corporations, and other entities that often have multimillion- to multibillion-dollar investments in real estate holdings. They often tend to hold their properties for long periods of time, and the IRR method gives them a better assessment of what type of return they can expect from a given property over a period of years.

The IRR method is usually calculated for at least a five-year period and calculates several things: the pretax cash flow of a property; the after-tax cash flow of a property, taking depreciation into account; and the overall return on the investment, including the reinvestment of the after-tax cash flows into optimum interest-bearing accounts.

The IRR method is usually calculated for at least a five-year period and calculates several things.

Property Valuation Methods and Tax Consequences **73**

If you take the courses offered by the National Association of REALTORS® Marketing Institute that qualify you for the Certified Commercial Investment Member (CCIM) designation, you will learn how to perform an IRR calculation and will receive all the necessary forms to calculate one. Several computer programs are now available that will perform the IRR calculation for you. The *Real Estate Investment Analysis V18* program offered by Real Data is highly touted and used by many commercial brokers.

In our discussion of the IRR method of evaluation, we touched on the pre- and after-tax consequences of real estate ownership. Let's take a few minutes here to talk about what you should know about real estate taxation and tax shelter issues.

Before 1986, investors enjoyed what was called the accelerated cost recovery system (ACRS) of depreciation allowance on their income taxes, which meant that anyone could buy an income property and depreciate it or write the cost of the improvements off on his/her income taxes over a 15-year period. In 1986, this all came to a screeching halt. David Stockman, treasury secretary in the Reagan administration, was responsible for what is referred to as the Tax Reform Act of 1986, and it has changed the landscape of investment real estate ownership ever since.

New rules were been put into place that you, as a real estate professional, need to be aware of. A limitation was placed on what is allowed as or who qualifies to take a depreciation allowance on an income tax return.

Below you will find facts and examples of limitations on various tax deductions and allowable uses of those deductions. Because the tax laws are always undergoing change, these facts and examples may *not* reflect the tax laws as they exist now, but the discussion does include scenarios and information that will make you familiar with and aware of the need to stay current on basic tax laws as they apply to real estate, though only in the most general form. *You are advised never to give tax information to clients and to refer them to proper tax counsel.*

74 Chapter 7

> New rules have been put into place that you, as a real estate professional, need to be aware of.

Investors who do not actively manage their property (active management includes hiring a property manager) are not allowed to shelter active income. Because investors have no management responsibilities in investments such as limited partnerships and REITs, the investor may not use such passive or "paper" losses to shelter active income.

As a real estate professional, you may use passive losses from investment property to offset other income without any limitations if you meet specific criteria, which include devoting at least 750 hours during the tax year to property management activities.

In a recent U.S. Supreme Court ruling, *D'Avanzo v. United States of America*, the Court ruled that Andrew M. D'Avanzo, who was not a real estate licensee, could not take advantage of unlimited depreciation allowances and was subject to the $25,000 limitation. D'Avanzo claimed that he managed his properties full time and was therefore a real estate professional even though he was not licensed as a real estate agent and that he should be eligible for the unlimited treatment licensees enjoy. The Court disagreed, holding that this allowance is limited to real estate professionals who meet the 750-hour annual test.

The improvements of residential real estate are currently written off over a 27.5-year period, and nonresidential property is written off over a 39-year period. Remember, you *must* deduct the land before making a depreciation calculation.

> Remember, you *must* deduct the land before making a depreciation calculation.

Property Valuation Methods and Tax Consequences **75**

For example, you are a qualified investor and you own a 20-unit multifamily property for which you paid $2 million, including your nonrecurring closing costs that also attach to your property's adjusted cost basis. The county assessor has the allocation of land-to-improvements on your tax bill at 25% land and 75% improvements, and so you use the same ratio.

To calculate the annual straight-line depreciation allowance that you could take as a deduction on your income tax return, you would take the following steps:

1. Compute the original cost basis (purchase price plus nonrecurring closing costs).

2. Add to this the total amount of any capital improvements you have made to the property.

3. Determine the allocation of land and improvements.

4. Deduct the value of the land.

5. Determine whether the property is residential or nonresidential. Use 27.5 years for residential and 39 years for nonresidential.

6. Using the federal tax table shown on the following page, find the month the property was put into service by the taxpayer. In this example, the property was put into service in September, so you would go to column 9 and the first year (row 1) to find the percentage figure of 1.061% (0.0161).

7. Compute the depreciation by multiplying the depreciable basis by the appropriate percentage found in the chart.

76   *Chapter 7*

Federal Tax Table for Depreciation of Real Property (%).

General Depreciation System Method: Straight line
Recovery Period: 27.5 years

The month in the first recovery year the property is placed in service:

Year	1	2	3	4	5	6	7	8	9	10	11	12
1	3.485	3.182	2.879	2.576	2.273	1.970	1.667	1.364	1.061	0.758	0.455	0.152
2–8	3.636	3.636	3.636	3.636	3.636	3.636	3.636	3.636	3.636	3.636	3.636	3.636

General Depreciation System Method: Straight line
Recovery Period: 39 years

The month in the first recovery year the property is placed into service:

1											
2.461	2.247	2.033	1.819	1.605	1.391	1.177	0.963	0.749	0.535	0.321	0.107
2–39											
2.564	2.564	2.564	2.564	2.564	2.564	2.564	2.564	2.564	2.564	2.564	2.564

$2,000,000 Property value (including nonrecurring closing costs) – $500,000 Land value (25% per assessor) = $1,500,000 Total depreciation allowed.

Use 27.5 years because the property is residential.

Because our example puts the property into service in September, go to line 1, column 9, of the 27.5-year chart. You see that the taxpayer could take 1.06%, or $15,915, of the cost of the improvements off his/her tax return in the first year of purchase. Each year thereafter a deduction of 3.636%, or $54,540, could be made, subject to the $25,000 limitation if applicable.

Each time you take a depreciation deduction on your income tax, you lower the "adjusted basis" of your property. If you subsequently sell your property, you will realize gain in two ways: You will realize a capital gain (you hope!) by way of the property's increase in value that will be taxed at the rate of 15% of the net gain

Property Valuation Methods and Tax Consequences **77**

(if you owned the property more than one year), and you will realize depreciation recapture that will be taxed at the rate of 25%. Depreciation recapture is the total amount of depreciation taken since you bought or exchanged into the current property. If you exchanged into it, then there may be additional depreciation recapture from previous property owned and exchanged into this one. *Always advise your clients in writing to consult a tax professional before selling an investment property to assess the tax consequences.*

If you are representing a client in the sale or exchange of one or more investment properties, you should always incorporate the following language into each purchase contract your client signs, for both the sale of the existing property and the purchase of the new one: "This sale is contingent on the written approval of the [here you insert the word "purchaser's" or "seller's"] tax and/or legal counsel within 10 days after final acceptance of this agreement."

Tax-Deferred Exchanges

The tax laws change constantly because our legislators tend to use them to effect social change, but at this writing the laws are very favorable to real estate. As stated previously, if a taxpayer has owned a property for more than one year, he/she can sell it and pay only 15% long-term capital gains tax. If, however, your client has already taken a depreciation allowance on it, he/she will also pay a "depreciation recapture" tax on the amount of depreciation taken. This tax is currently at a 25% tax rate, and so if your client is going to reinvest in other investment real estate, he/she should consider making a tax-deferred exchange for the new property acquisition to avoid paying a capital gains tax.

It is no longer necessary for the properties involved in a tax-deferred exchange to close escrow simultaneously. Under the current tax ruling, a taxpayer may do a "Starker" delayed exchange if he/she so chooses (see the bulleted example for a detailed explanation).

78   *Chapter 7*

"Simultaneous closings" and "direct deeding" used to be allowed, but in recent years the Internal Revenue Service (IRS) obtained a revenue ruling that states that a qualified "intermediary" must be used for a tax-deferred exchange; otherwise, the IRS will disallow it. An intermediary is a qualified third party that acts as an escrow holder for the taxpayer's property or cash so that the taxpayer does not receive "constructive receipt" of either and have his/her exchange disallowed.

It works like this:

- Your client sells property A, subject to a tax-deferred exchange. An escrow is opened and an intermediary is named. Your client begins looking for a replacement property.

- Escrow closes and your client deeds property A to the intermediary, who then deeds it to the buyer. The cash proceeds from the sale of property A are given to the intermediary by the escrow company or closing attorney at closing and are held on behalf of your client until a replacement property (B) is found. Easy enough, but there is a timing issue to deal with. Your client must "name," in writing, the property or properties he/she is going to acquire. No more than three properties may be named, and the aggregate total of the value of the named properties may not exceed three times the value of property A; otherwise, the exchange may be disallowed. Your client has 45 days after close of escrow of property A to name the new property (property B) and the earlier of 180 days after close of property A or until the end of the next tax reporting period to close the exchange escrow; otherwise, the exchange may be disallowed.

- Your client finds a replacement property he/she likes. You make an offer on it for the client and it is accepted, subject to a tax-deferred exchange.

Property Valuation Methods and Tax Consequences **79**

- The exchange escrow is opened, and your client assigns his/her rights in that purchase contract to the intermediary. At closing, the intermediary turns over your client's sale proceeds from property A to the escrow company or closing attorney.

- The exchange escrow closes, and property B is deeded to the intermediary, who immediately deeds the property to your client through the exchange escrow.

If your client goes equal or up in value and loans, he/she does not receive any "boot," and the exchange is totally tax deferred. If your client receives cash, personal property, or mortgage relief through the exchange escrow, whatever is received is taxable. (Obtaining a loan on the newly acquired property that is less than the one the investor had on the demised property will result in a tax on the difference between the old and new loan.)

It is beyond the scope of this book to teach you about all tax-deferred exchanges, but if you are going to be working in the commercial real estate arena, they will be an ever-present part of your life, and you should therefore take classes that teach you more about them. The Women's Counsel of REALTORS® (WCR) and most of the title companies sponsor classes on tax-deferred exchanges from time to time, so contact your favorite title representative, real estate association, or local WCR chapter for more information.

Internal Revenue Code Section 1031, which deals with tax-deferred exchanges, is actually very small. It is the subsequent tax court decisions that give such weight and meaning to what may or may not be done. The more you know about them, the higher the degree of professional service and advice you can give. I would especially advise you to learn about the *Biggs* decision, the *Mercantile Trust* decision, and the *Starker* decision, which were handed down by the tax court, because they are the basis for much of the real estate tax law that exists today.

80 *Chapter 7*

Review Questions

1. An eligible owner will depreciate his/her neighborhood retail shopping center over how many years?
   A. 39
   B. 27.5
   C. 40
   D. varies with the age of the buildings

2. Erin Chase has asked you to sell her 80-unit multifamily property, which she has owned for 16 years. What is one of the most important questions you should ask her?
   A. How much do you feel the property is worth?
   B. What is the building's age?
   C. Are the units air conditioned?
   D. Will you be acquiring a replacement property?

3. Fred says to you, "What will my capital gains tax be if I decide not to reinvest?" What should you ask or tell him?
   A. What is the adjusted basis of your property?
   B. How much depreciation have you taken?
   C. That's a tax question, and you should consul your tax counsel.
   D. both A and B answer choices

4. Retail strip centers in the midtown area are selling at an average cap rate of 7.4%. You have been asked to list one that is 50% vacant and has a lot of deferred maintenance the owner says he is not willing to repair. What cap rate are you likely to use?
   A. a higher one
   B. a lower one
   C. the average for the area
   D. any of the answer choices (The choice really doesn't matter.)

Property Valuation Methods and Tax Consequences 81

5. A building is appraised at $2.75 million. What is its NOI at a 7.2% cap rate?
   A. $175,000
   B. $147,000
   C. $198,000
   D. $189,000

Class Discussion Topics

1. John B has asked you to sell his 12-unit multifamily property. What questions should you ask him?
2. Madeline H is the managing partner and sole beneficiary of an LLC that owns the land and building leased to a McDonald's Restaurant franchisee on an NNN lease. Can she take a depreciation allowance every year, and if so, how much per year after the first year? What advice would you give her?
3. An investor has asked Jerry L to evaluate the value of a 404-unit self-storage facility and to advise him as to what price he should offer. What are the issues that may affect the value of the property?
4. Your client has fully executed a purchase contract with a buyer who is represented by another agent for the purchase and sale of her retail building, and she wishes to make a tax-deferred exchange for a NNN-leased restaurant. She was very dissatisfied with the other agent's service and wants you to represent her in acquiring the restaurant. What clauses should be in the purchase contract and counteroffer? What questions should you be asking her?
5. Describe the entire process of fully executing a proper and complete tax-deferred exchange from start to finish. If the taxpayer is financing the new acquisition, who and/or what entities are involved, and why?

Chapter 8

The Annual Business Plan

84   *Chapter 8*

Month 1

1. Find where and when the next class on Section 1031 tax-deferred exchanges is and sign up to attend.

2. Re-read Part 2 of this book and decide which type or types of commercial real estate you want to specialize in.

3. Set a budget for your monthly mailings. If you are working for a large commercial firm, expect the firm to pay for your postage and materials; if, however, you are working for a residential firm or a small commercial firm, you will probably have to pay the cost of postage and supplies yourself. Sixty cents per mailing should cover the cost of commercial stationery, envelopes, ink for your computer, and first-class postage. But be careful: Do not use bulk mail; it immediately sends the wrong message to the recipient, and many people just find it offensive. These potential clients are going to make you many thousands of dollars, and so they are all worth the monthly cost of a first-class stamp.

4. Have your favorite title company get you as detailed a printout as you can get of every one of the commercial properties you are going to specialize in and give it to you in such a fashion that you can place it in an electronic database. If it is downloadable directly as an Excel file or in some other convenient manner, it will save you hours of computer time.

5. With your list in hand, plan to spend at least two hours a day driving by and taking a digital picture of every property in your database. Stop at each property to get as much information about it as you can (e.g., retail tenants of a retail center, number of units of an apartment complex, etc.).

6. Research the owners or contact person of each property through the county assessor's records, CoStar, or LoopNet.

The Annual Business Plan   85

You will find that most properties today are owned by limited liability companies (LLCs) or corporations. You need the name of a person of authority to mail to, so if you encounter LLCs or corporations, go to the state's secretary of state website to search by the LLC or corporation's name. You will see a managing partner identified for an LLC. This is most often the owner or one of the owners who has been given the authority to act for the LLC. A corporation will also name someone. Those are the names you want in your database. Be sure to update your list every six months and each time you list or sell one of the properties.

7. Write an introductory letter to send to each contact person to tell him/her who you are, the name of your company, and what you are attempting to do (i.e., expand your client base by meeting potential clients and providing a service for them so that they will come to know you and hopefully use your services when they need investment real estate help now or at a later date). Send a page of Sold or For Sale comparative properties (comps) with your letter. People love getting these, and it will make them hang on to your mail. I have met people for the first time, three years after I started my mail campaign, and they would proudly show me a complete file of my mailings!

8. Call each contact person two or three days after you have sent your introductory letter. Tell your contacts you are calling to see if they received your letter and ask if they will allow you to include them in your database so that you can send them regular information about commercial real estate in the local community and a quarterly rental survey.

   NOTE: After each phone contact you make, no matter what the outcome is, send the contact person a handwritten thank-you note for the time he/she spent with you. This is a critical step.

86   *Chapter 8*

9. Make a decision about how you are going to approach your commercial real estate career—will you continue residential real estate brokerage while you transition to commercial brokerage or will you work for a commercial firm right away.

NOTE: If you join a large commercial firm, plan on prospecting at least five hours a day every day, six days a week. You will also spend approximately two hours a day researching contact persons for each property and two hours a day "driving the territory." If you are transitioning to commercial real estate, you should "time block" an hour or two each day to engage in these activities; increase the time spent on commercial real estate slowly as you fill up the hour or two you have time blocked each day, until you have made a gradual but complete transition.

Re-read Part 2 of this book and decide which type or types of commercial real estate you want to specialize in.

Month 2

1. Continue to drive your marketing area and take pictures of properties.

2. Start to build a comparable sales book (the comp book) either in hard copy in an attractive three-ring binder or electronically on your laptop. This book will be broken down and tabbed by city; then, each city will be broken down by sold price in either ascending or descending order. Use plastic holders for each comp so that each may be readily moved around as you get new comps. Each page should have a picture of the property and whatever data (e.g., address; sold price; cost per square foot, per-unit cost, and cost per acre) you feel are important comparison points.

The Annual Business Plan **87**

3. Start to prepare your listing proposal book. This book will be what you show potential sellers and will include information about your company and about you, including any letters of reference (They are gold!), your marketing plan, a reference to your comp book (which you will take with you on listing proposal meetings), and your estimate of the property's value and how you arrived at it, which should always be the last item in your proposal.

4. Research contact persons for each property.

5. Send introductory letters to contact persons.

6. Make follow-up telephone calls to contact persons to introduce yourself.

7. Research what investment groups, such as the local Certified Commercial Investment Member (CCIM) chapter, or commercial broker meetings are available in your community, and plan to join and attend regularly. These will give you a forum to present your new commercial listings to other commercial real estate professionals, let you in on new commercial listings that are available, and start to build your credibility within the existing commercial broker network that exists in your city or metropolitan area.

8. Check with your local, state, and national associations' education departments to see what they have to offer in the way of educational materials you can buy to learn more about commercial real estate. Buy at least three publications a year.

9. Refine your listing proposal book.

10. Drive by any new listings you hear about, and call to get information on them.

88   *Chapter 8*

NOTE: The informational package the listing broker puts together is referred to as a "setup." Each time you get a set-up on a property, be sure to update your database.

Start to prepare your listing proposal book.

Month 3

1. Continue to drive your market area, taking pictures of the properties you are specializing in, to gain as much knowledge about each property as you can.

2. Continue to build your comp book.

3. Send out any first-time letters to new contact persons.

4. Call contact persons to introduce yourself. Send thank-you notes.

5. Attend the CCIM chapter meeting. Get to know people, present your listings, and hear about new listings.

6. Refine your listing proposal book.

7. Drive by any new listings, and call and get a setup on them.

8. Get the names of two well-referred property management agents and leasing agents who specialize in your type of commercial property. Call them and offer to take them to lunch as a get-acquainted gesture. Ask them about current rental rates and vacancy rates in the area you service.

9. Conduct a rental survey.

The Annual Business Plan   89

NOTE: The results of your rental survey are very well received by the property owners and contact persons you meet, and these results are an excellent reason to call them to see if they would like to receive a quarterly report from you. People love getting these!

10. Conduct listing proposal appointments and show property as needed.

> Conduct a rental survey.

Month 4

1. Drive the area and continue to add properties to your database.

2. Continue to build your comp book.

3. Research new contact persons for properties entered into your database.

4. Send introductory letters to contact persons.

5. Make follow-up phone calls to new contact persons.

6. Make follow-up calls to any contact persons who have expressed an interest in buying or selling.

7. Refine your listing proposal book.

8. Attend the local CCIM chapter meeting.

9. Drive by any new listings you hear about; call and get a setup on them.

90   *Chapter 8*

10. Conduct listing proposal appointments and show property as required.

11. Initiate and send out your quarterly newsletter with your rental survey results.

Month 5

1. Drive your area and continue to take pictures of properties to add to your database. Stop to obtain available "for lease" information on them as well.

2. Update your comp book.

3. Research the names of contact persons and send them your initial letters.

4. Make follow-up telephone calls to new contact persons. Send thank-you notes.

5. Check in with existing clients to see what they need.

6. Attend a commercial real estate seminar. (CI 101 is a good example of an excellent class to attend because it will start you on the road to your CCIM designation and thoroughly teach you how to use a programmable calculator. I also recommend either the HP-12C or the HP-10B.)

7. Attend the local CCIM chapter meeting.

8. Drive by any new listings you hear about; call and get a set-up on them.

9. Conduct listing proposal appointments and show property as required.

Month 6

1. Add properties to your database.

2. Update your comp book.

3. If you have finished completing your database, start to double-check it for accuracy. For retail properties, this will entail driving your territory all over again to check for vacancy signs and new retail tenants. For apartment complexes and self-storage facilities, this will mean verifying that the same resident manager is still there.

4. Drive by any new listings you have heard about and call to ask for a setup.

5. Drive by, take a picture, and gather information on new properties for your database.

6. Call your leasing or property management contact for lunch. Ask about current rental rates and vacancy factors.

7. Call your existing clients to see what help they need.

8. Conduct your quarterly rental survey.

9. Attend the local CCIM chapter meeting.

10. Conduct listing proposal appointments and show property as required.

Month 7

1. Drive your territory and refine your database.

2. Update your comp book.

92   *Chapter 8*

3. Contact all your existing clients to see what help they need.

4. Contact any new property owners you have entered into your database.

5. Update your database (recheck the current contact person's or owner's name).

6. Attend the local CCIM chapter meeting.

7. Drive by any new listings, and call and get a setup.

8. Update your listing proposal book (add new letters of reference, etc.).

9. Send out your quarterly newsletter with your latest rental survey results.

10. Conduct listing proposal appointments and show property as required.

Month 8

1. Drive your territory. Look for new properties to add to your database. Look for new property management signs and new tenants if you are engaging in retail brokerage.

2. Update your comp book.

3. Call as many contact persons in your database as you can. See if they are getting your newsletter, and ask if they need help with any of their property. Send each one you talk with a thank-you note.

4. Attend a local seminar on investment property.

The Annual Business Plan 93

5. Attend the local CCIM chapter meeting.

6. Drive by any new listings you hear about. Get a setup on them and update your database.

7. Call your existing and past clients to see if they need any help from you. Ask how they like your newsletter.

8. Conduct listing proposal appointments and show property as required.

9. Take a week-long vacation.

Month 9

1. Drive your territory.

2. If you see any new construction of the type of property you specialize in, get the names of the developers. Write to them; then, call to see if you can have lunch or coffee with them. Let them know that you are an experienced commercial agent who specializes in their type of property. Ask them to consider you the next time they need brokerage services. Ask permission to put them on your mailing list, and tell them about your quarterly rental survey.

3. Update your comp book. Take any new pictures that you need to.

4. Call and have lunch with your property management or leasing agent contacts. Get any new vacancy rate or rental rate information from them that you can. Be prepared to update them on the state of the sales market as well.

5. Attend the local CCIM chapter luncheon. Present your listings.

94   *Chapter 8*

6. Conduct listing proposal appointments and show property as required.

7. Send out introductory letters to any new contact persons or new owners.

8. Call contact persons and/or owners to keep in touch. Ask if they have any need for your services and whether they are still getting your newsletter with the rental survey.

9. Drive by any new listings. Take a picture if you don't already have one. Call and get a setup, and change the information in your comps and your database.

10. Conduct your quarterly rental survey.

11. Conduct listing proposal meetings and show property as required.

Month 10

1. Recheck your database to see that it is current. Make any changes that are necessary.

2. Send out introductory letters to any new owners.

3. Call your database contacts and introduce yourself to the new ones. Ask if they received your letter and whether they would like to be put on your list to receive your quarterly newsletter with your rental survey. Send each person you talk with a handwritten thank-you note.

4. Send out your newsletter to your database and call a few days later to see if your clients and potential clients received it. Ask if they need any help with their property. Send thank-you notes as appropriate.

The Annual Business Plan 95

5. Drive by any new listings you have heard about. Get a setup and make changes in your database.

6. Update your listing proposal book as necessary.

7. Update your comp book.

8. Conduct listing proposal meetings and show property as required.

Month 11

1. Drive your territory. Look at your properties, checking for any new construction or any new property management firms, leasing companies, or developers you have found. Call each of them and introduce yourself as a commercial agent who specializes in their type of property and ask if you may be of any help. Ask if they would like to be put on your mailing list to receive your quarterly newsletter and your rental survey.

2. Update your comp book.

3. Update your listing proposal as required. Indicate the properties where you have represented the buyer or seller.

4. Drive by any new listings. Get a setup, and update your comp book and database.

5. Attend the local CCIM chapter meeting. Present your listings, and make note of any new ones presented by other brokers.

6. Conduct listing proposal meetings and show property as required.

96   *Chapter 8*

Month 12

1. Early in the month, send out "Happy Holiday" cards to as many people in your database as you feel is appropriate.

2. Call your property management and leasing agent contacts to arrange lunch, preferably with both of them. Get the latest news from them about vacancy rates and any changes in rental rates. Tell them about any new sale-related changes you have become aware of.

3. Drive the territory and note any changes. Make introductory calls to any new property management firms, leasing companies, or developers. If you are engaging in retail brokerage, note any new tenants.

4. Attend the local CCIM chapter meeting if one is being held this month. Present your listings, get setups on new listings, and make the necessary changes in your comp book and your database.

5. Make as many calls as you can to your database, especially your existing clients, to ask if they need year-end help with any of their properties.

6. Arrange a day to get away someplace quiet to create your next year's business plan. Each year should have increasingly more activities listed each month that are directed toward a particular person with whom you have been creating a relationship. Be sure to include vacations and time for those close to you as well as for continuing education classes.

7. Conduct listing proposal meetings and show property as required.

The Annual Business Plan 97

8. Complete a thorough year-end assessment of your database. Delete anyone you feel has become unproductive, and look for any changes you missed throughout the year. Make special note of anyone you feel will be productive for you this next year, and in your appointment book, make a special notation to contact that person at what you feel is an appropriate time next year.

9. Take a good look at your comp book to check that it is up to date.

10. Assess your workload to see if it may be nearing time for you to hire either a part-time or a full-time licensed assistant.

Review Questions

1. What is a productive thing you can do in your first month as a commercial agent?
   A. take a course on Internal Revenue Code Section 1031 tax-deferred exchanges
   B. create a marketing budget
   C. create and refine an annual business plan
   D. all of the answer choices

2. What is an effective way to meet commercial property owners?
   A. research and constantly refine a database of owners of the type of property you are specializing in
   B. send them an introductory letter and comps first, and a short letter about market conditions and comps each month after
   C. call them to ask if they received your mailing and whether they need your brokerage services at this time
   D. all of the answer choices

98   *Chapter 8*

3. What should be included in your first mailing to your commercial property database?
    A. recent For Sale offerings and Sold comps
    B. an introductory letter, current listings, and Sold comps
    C. your résumé, an introductory letter, current listings, and Sold comps
    D. all of the answer choices

4. Which of the following statements about taking digital pictures of properties is NOT true?
    A. When received by the owner, the picture suggests that you are enthusiastic and detail oriented.
    B. In talking with the owner, you can use the picture as an effective conversation piece.
    C. Taking pictures of a property violates the owner's privacy.
    D. You should take a digital picture of every property in your database.

5. What is the primary importance of creating a business plan?
    A. It lets you work efficiently on the most important task at any given time.
    B. Because it is focused, it saves you gas money.
    C. It allows you to include important nonbusiness activities.
    D. It allows you to preplan vacations.

Class Discussion Topics

1. You are new to commercial real estate brokerage and are putting your annual business plan together for the following year. In order of importance, what are the items you need to be sure to schedule?
2. What items should be included in the introductory letter you will send out to your commercial database, and why?
3. Discuss the pros and cons of using a laptop instead of a three-ring binder for your comp sales book. If you use a laptop,

should you back up your information on a thumb drive or disc, and if so, why?

4. What are the advantages of driving the areas where your database properties are located? Does this give you an edge over your competition? Why?

5. What advantages, if any, do you gain by developing a good relationship with a leasing agent and a property manager who specialize in the same type of property as you do?

Chapter 9

The Listing Proposal

102   *Chapter 9*

This chapter describes two topics: the types of listing agreements you may end up working with and the listing proposal itself.

There are four types of listings that may be offered to you:

- exclusive authorization and right-to-sell listing

- exclusive agency listing

- open listing

- verbal listing

The only type of listing that offers you any reasonable assurance that you will be paid if the property sells is the *exclusive authorization and right to sell.* This type of listing is a mirror image of what is most commonly used in residential real estate. It states that you are the sole listing agent or agency and that you get paid no matter who represents the buyer in the purchase of the property. You will find many owners of commercial property resistant to entering into this type of listing with you unless you and your firm are well known to them. This type of listing is used almost exclusively by the large commercial real estate firms.

> The only type of listing that offers you any reasonable assurance that you will be paid if the property sells is the *exclusive authorization and right to sell.*

The *exclusive agency listing* states that you are the exclusive listing agent and agency. However, the owner reserves the right to sell the property himself/herself to people with whom you have not had negotiations, and the owner owes you and your firm no commission if he/she is successful at selling the property himself/herself. It's easy to see the inherent problems with this type of listing. You and your firm could end up spending a lot of time and money marketing a property, only to have the seller find his/her own buyer. It's relatively easy for other real estate agents to go around you and make side deals with the owner so that they get a larger commission. In addition, if the owner is actively marketing the property, it can be very confusing for investors who see your ads as well as the owner's. The owner may even offer the same property at a lower price, and if your buyer happens across such an ad, it can hurt your credibility.

An *open listing* is in writing and sets the price and terms, but it states that it is cancelable "at will" and gives you no protection at all, except for tying down the price and terms. An open listing may be entered into with more than one broker at a time because it doesn't give any one broker the authority to act as the exclusive agent of the seller. Many sellers of commercial real estate will offer this type of listing only to an agent or agency they don't know personally. Their main fear is that the property will be tied up for a period of time and that the agent or broker will not perform diligently. The drawback to you is that you could end up spending a lot of time and money finding a buyer only to have the seller decline your offer and look for others or even go to your buyer directly and leave you out of the equation.

The last type of listing (or nonlisting) is the *verbal listing*, also known as a "pocket listing." In this instance, the property owner tells you verbally that you may work on the property and that he/ she wants a certain price for it. The owner may also just tell you to bring offers and not even quote you a price. You don't want to get caught up in this type of quasi-marketing of someone's property. Even if the owner has quoted you a price, there is nothing binding about it. Let's say you represent the property to an investor as being available at a certain price. He likes the property and makes a really good offer that you take to the owner. The owner looks at

104   *Chapter 9*

your offer and says that she has changed her mind and doesn't want to sell any longer or that she may sell if you get your buyer to increase his offer considerably. You and the buyer you are representing have very little, if any, bargaining power, and your credibility with your client has suffered greatly. You may even lose that person as a client.

> If an owner wants to give you a verbal or open listing, what should you do?

If an owner wants to give you a verbal or open listing, what should you do?

First, have a standard that you work by. Include in your standard that you will not work on anything but an exclusive authorization to sell. If someone offers you anything other than an exclusive authorization to sell listing, question why and address the owner's fears. As I stated earlier, the main reluctance to give you an exclusive is that you or your firm will not perform. When I was working in commercial real estate in the Bay Area, I got this type of resistance regularly. I overcame it by having a highly detailed marketing and advertising plan with me when I met with the owners to discuss taking their listing. I would offer to make the marketing plan an addendum to the listing agreement. It stated that in the event I did not perform each and every item in the agreement as stated, the owners only needed to give me notice of the breach; and if I did not cure the breach within 24 hours of their notification, they could cancel the listing. This approach didn't get me every listing, but it got me plenty!

NOTE: The amount of commission or fee charged is set between the property owners and the brokerage firm. There is no such thing as a fixed commission.

Listing Proposal

Now let's discuss the listing proposal itself. What exactly is it, how long should it be for, and what does it contain that a residential listing agreement doesn't have?

I discussed earlier in this chapter the types of listings that are available. You will have to set your own standard as to the type of listing you are willing to work with. If you go to work for a large commercial brokerage firm, its standard will dictate, and you will almost certainly be working on, exclusive authorizations only.

The firm you work for will probably have its own version of a listing proposal or presentation. Many of these are really fine pieces of work, whereas some others need help. The large commercial firm I worked for in Phoenix had a generic listing proposal that was a multipage PowerPoint product that could be altered as to comps and other details and be presented electronically or printed out and used in hard-copy format.

If your firm doesn't have a listing proposal for you, then you will need to create one. I suggest that you start with a 1-inch, three-ring binder; you can obtain one at any office supply store or create a binder on your laptop. You will then need to break it down into sections.

Section 1 should contain a few pages about the company you work for. It should tell the sellers what the company is all about in as few pages as it takes to get the full message out. Too many pages in this section can become tedious to read and make the sellers lose interest. As you start to go through this proposal with the sellers, keep in mind that everyone listens to the same favorite radio station—that is, station WIIFM, or "What's in it for me?" Each time you present a page in your listing proposal, be prepared to present the benefit that is tied to it. People do not really care

106   *Chapter 9*

about features, except when they are tied to something that benefits them.

Section 2 should have your résumé and photocopies of any professional designations or college diplomas you care to share with the sellers. Again, present your credentials as a feature tied to a benefit to the sellers.

Section 3 could be titled "What People Are Saying about Me" and should contain any letters you have received from satisfied customers. You should make a habit of asking for testimonials of this type after every transaction; they are worth their weight in gold. You can expect the sellers to stop everything and actually read at least some of these, and it is interesting to watch the expression on their faces as they do. This is essentially a third-party sell of your credibility and skills.

Section 4 will have your marketing and advertising plan clearly stated. Be as detailed as you can, even laying out what will occur on a weekly basis. It should clearly spell out where you are going to advertise and when, what type of brochure you are going to create (provide an example), and to whom you are going to distribute the brochures and how often. It should tell sellers how often you will see them personally as well as call them to update them on showings and interest from the public and from other brokers. It should call for monthly meetings to discuss the pricing strategy in the event of no offers.

Section 5 should have the appropriate comparable sales (comps) from your comp book (as an alternative, you can just take your comp book with you, with the appropriate comps tabbed for easy access). You will also include the worksheet that shows how you arrived at your recommended asking and final sales prices, as well as a sheet that formally spells out your pricing strategy—that is, what you recommend as an asking price and the low and high recommended final sales prices.

NOTE: This listing proposal book, done properly, is a huge step in building the kind of trust in you the client will need to agree to give you an exclusive authorization listing, so take the time to make a really good one.

> This listing proposal book, done properly, is a huge step in building the kind of trust in you the client will need to agree to give you an exclusive authorization listing.

Now that you have created the listing proposal, let's talk a little bit about the actual presentation of your material to the potential sellers.

Presentation

Everyone is different, and you will need to learn to size people up quickly to work with each one in a manner that each finds agreeable. If you go into a meeting and spend a lot of time making small talk with a type A personality, this person will almost certainly not list with you and may just throw you out. You *will* have many type A's in your database. When you interact with them, be "business polite" and to the point; they will really appreciate your directness. If, however, you are dealing with a person who is into relationships, you will need to spend more time with "familiarization talk." These types really want to know about the person they are dealing with on a more personal level. There is no way to teach this skill; you will just learn it as you go along. If you err toward the latter type of interaction, with an eye or ear for signs of "Let's get to it," you will soon develop great skill at reading people's preferences.

You may very well already have taken a picture of a type A's property; if not, be sure that you do so as a part of your proposal. After the settling-in stage, compliment the person on his/her property if it is appropriate to do so (I can remember talking at length to a representative of a REIT about a retail shopping center in Apache Junction, Arizona, that had absolutely no redeemable qualities). If you don't know the person's plans regarding a tax-deferred exchange or sale, ask what he/she proposes to do with the sale proceeds and if you may be of any help in finding replacement property. Once you know the seller's strategy, ask for permission to go through your proposal with him/her. It is a good idea to tell the seller about how long it will take and what it contains.

As you go through each section, keep an eye on the seller to see that he/she is still with you. Look for body language, voice inflection, and any other sign of boredom or sign that the seller isn't buying in to what you are putting forth. When you get to the comps, always say, "The market shows that . . .," instead of having the data come from you. This way, if the seller doesn't like the price you recommend, you can make it the market's fault and not yours. Plan to spend a lot of time explaining your marketing plan and how you arrived at the value you have placed on the property. These are the two areas sellers will be the most focused on, and if they are presented correctly, you will have a good shot at getting the listing.

> When you get to the comps, always say, "The market shows that . . .," instead of having the data come from you.

If, during the course of your presentation, you want to test the water to see if sellers are ready to list with you, you may want to state, "At some point I'll need a copy of your leases" or "Will you allow me to put a sign on the property?" Their reaction to open-ended questions or statements like these will often tell where they are with regard to listing with you.

The Listing Proposal 109

When you are through with your presentation, ask the sellers if there is anything they would like you to go over again or any other information they need that you haven't supplied them with. These questions show sellers your penchant for thoroughness that sellers like to see, and these will often bring out any hidden objections that haven't been addressed yet.

A good final question is always "How do you feel about having [firm name] and me represent you?"

Review Questions

1. Which of the following statements about property sales is NOT true ?
   A. The commission is set by the local real estate association in the area.
   B. The commission is negotiated between the property owners and the brokerage firm.
   C. The agent taking the listing must take whatever commission the sellers dictate.
   D. both A and C answer choices

2. A developer gives you an open listing on 175 acres of land, and you bring him a full-price offer at the price and terms he quoted. How much commission does he owe you if he doesn't sign the purchase agreement?
   A. none
   B. the amount he quoted you during your discussion
   C. the customary commission for land sales in your area
   D. just 10% (Land is always 10%.)

3. What is every seller's favorite radio station, and what do the letters stand for?
   A. Station WIFFM. What's in favor for me?
   B. Station WIIFM. What's in it for me?
   C. Station WIFMM. What's in front of my module?
   D. Station WIIFY. What's in it for you?

110   *Chapter 9*

4. What is the appropriate way to share market information on the property's value with the sellers?
   A. "By looking at these comparable properties, the market appears to indicate that your property is worth...."
   B. "My opinion is that your property is worth...."
   C. "I'm sure you can see that my assessment of the property's value is correct."
   D. "What do you feel we should list your property at?"

5. When presenting your listing proposal, it is wise to pay close attention to what?
   A. your client's body language and nonverbal communication
   B. that the room temperature is comfortable
   C. how often the client's spouse interrupts him/her
   D. all of the answer choices

Class Discussion Topics

1. Describe the four types of property listings and discuss the advantages and disadvantages of each one to you and to the seller.
2. You have been nurturing a potential shopping center listing for three months. The owners finally call you and ask you to meet them at noon tomorrow. You go through your entire listing proposal with them, and the owners tell you they are willing to give you an exclusive agency listing only because they may have an interested party. What do you do?
3. Describe the five sections of a listing proposal and explain the importance of each one.
4. You are at a listing appointment, and you have reached the "value" part. When the husband sees the price range you have recommended, he crosses his arms and turns away from you with a scowl on his face. How will you handle this?
5. Name as many "trial closes" as you can and tell the class why you think each will work.

Chapter 10

Advertising and Marketing Commercial Real Estate

112   *Chapter 10*

Although similar in nature, marketing and advertising are actually somewhat different. Marketing is more about "branding," or making a name for a person or product, whereas advertising is more about getting a target audience interested in a specific product or service.

Advertising

Advertising commercial real estate is different from advertising residential real estate. Commercial real estate investors don't go to open houses and seldom go into real estate offices looking for good investments to buy. They read the papers and go to the Internet, and many tend to rely heavily on their real estate broker.

If you are using the newspaper for your advertising, be sure to pick the correct paper. The local papers are not usually where investors spend much time; they opt for the larger regional newspapers that are more likely to have a greater number of investment properties listed in a separate commercial section. Because the investor will not be living in the investment, he/she will consider owning real estate farther away from where he/she lives as long as it is managed properly. Nearly all agents who sell land or industrial property advertise their listings in magazines and other publications that deal with those specific types of property only. They are widely read by land developers and those who buy and sell industrial property. If you specialize in either of these types of property, ask an experienced agent in your office or your broker about the names of these publications.

> Because the investor will not be living in the investment, he/she will consider owning real estate farther away from where he/she lives.

Newspaper advertising is expensive, especially if you are using the *Wall Street Journal, USA Today,* or even one of the larger regional papers like the *San Francisco Examiner,* but such papers are also the most effective ones to use if you are selling a property that warrants that kind of exposure. Because of the cost, you will want to keep your ad as small as possible while conveying enough information to make someone want to call you. People don't read newspaper ads—they scan them—so it is very important to follow the time-tested AIDA formula when you create an ad:

Attention—you need to get the reader to stop scanning and instead actually read your ad.

Interest—the first few words of your ad need to gain the reader's interest and make him/her want to read the rest of the ad.

Desire—the rest of your ad needs to create a desire for more information and a desire to call you.

Action—the last part of your ad needs to urge the reader to take action, to call you for an appointment or for more information. Here's an example:

WELL-LOCATED GARDEN APARTMENTS

Excellent San Francisco suburb area with almost no vacancy.

80 garden units. Almost all 2-BR units. Long-term tenants.

6.5% cap rate.

$20 million or your property in trade.

Don't miss this excellent investment—call Bob Herd at 520-555-1010.

---

114   *Chapter 10*

This style of ad tells the reader several things:

- approximately where the property is without disclosing the exact location;

- the price of the property;

- the return at the list price;

- that the owner may take the reader's property in trade (if the owner doesn't want the reader's property, you as the broker would list the reader's property if it isn't already listed, and you would seek a buyer for a normal three-way exchange); and

- to act now by calling you for more information.

Be careful not to make your ad so small (to save money) that you turn it into an ineffective ad that won't get you any calls. Doing so is penny wise and pound foolish.

If you are new or newer at the commercial real estate business, call a few commercial brokers in your area to ask them where they get the best results from newspaper advertising.

> Be careful not to make your ad so small (to save money) that you turn it into an ineffective ad that won't get you any calls. Doing so is penny wise and pound foolish.

The Internet

Every day more and more commercial brokers are using the Internet to advertise their listings. Your Internet site must achieve

Advertising and Marketing Commercial Real Estate 115

the same results as the newspapers if you are to receive bona fide client enquiries. Your site must contain enough information to get an investor interested but omit just enough to make the investor call you.

If you would like to see an excellent Internet site, I suggest you go to eMarket at www.propertyline.com/market/emarket. Commercial broker Mark Goldberg, with MID-AMERICA Real Estate Corporation, has several of his listings featured there, and they contain just enough information to get him calls from interested investors. The site has a great format.

CoStar is an online national commercial database that lists every type of commercial real estate from every state. It is not inexpensive; if you are an active commercial agent with listings to sell and investors to represent, however, it is a must-have. It gives traffic counts, square feet of the properties and the land they are on, income/expense data, capitalization (cap) rates, and so much more. LoopNet is another commercial site that is somewhat less expensive than CoStar, but LoopNet was purchased by CoStar, and the two databases will be merged soon.

If you work for a commercial real estate firm, it may provide you with a webpage on its website. If so, create your webpage with care and always make directing the client to call or contact you the main goal of your website.

Marketing

As I said earlier, the lines are sometimes blurred between advertising and marketing. In addition to using newspaper ads and the Internet, consider joining as many of the commercial real estate groups in your area as you can. Plan to attend their monthly marketing meetings as often as you can, even if you don't have a listing to sell.

116   *Chapter 10*

These meetings regularly include educational sessions where you will learn things you just can't learn elsewhere. They also run marketing sessions where commercial agents match buyers with sellers and put transactions together. These meetings are also a great place to get to know the other commercial agents in your area.

At this time there are almost no viable commercial multiple listing services (MLS) in the United States, with the exception of CoStar, LoopNet, and a few others. Commercial agents just won't put their inventory in them because too many totally unqualified residential agents try to work on them, with horrible results. If you attend the local Certified Commercial Investment Member (CCIM) chapter meetings and other commercial meetings, you will get to know the players; once you gain their trust and respect, they will gladly share their inventory with you when you have a buyer.

> If you attend the local CCIM chapter meetings and other commercial meetings, you will get to know the players.

Review Questions

1. Which newspapers get the best print advertising results?
   A. local throwaways
   B. large regional papers
   C. specialty papers
   D. all of the answer choices

2. What is the main purpose of advertising?
   A. tell a story about you that will attract clients
   B. create an image in the reader's or viewer's mind about your company
   C. attract other commercial agents to want to work with you
   D. sell a specific product or service

Advertising and Marketing Commercial Real Estate 117

3. What is the main purpose of marketing?
   A. tell a story about you and your company that will encourage readers or viewers to contact you
   B. sell a land listing you have
   C. get the word out about a new listing you just got
   D. both B and C answer choices

4. Other than CoStar, what method(s) can you use to advertise your listings?
   A. mailing flyers to owners of like-kind property in the area of your listings
   B. attending CCIM chapter lunches in your area and talking about your listings
   C. holding an open house on a vacant apartment unit
   D. both A and B answer choices

5. You are looking for a specific type of property to sell but haven't found it on any of the commercial databases. Which of the following is an effective way to learn about off-market properties?
   A. call agents you know who specialize in that type of property to see if they know of any available
   B. attend the local CCIM chapter meeting, and in the open forum period ask if anyone knows of the availability of that type of property
   C. ask residential agents you know to keep a sharp eye out for that type of property for you
   D. both A and B answer choices

Class Discussion Topics

1. Why are commercial property owners willing to invest in properties far away from where they live, and how important is effective property management to this decision?
2. What type of property information should be included in all your advertising? What should be omitted?

118   *Chapter 10*

3. What are the advantages of following the AIDA formula in your advertising?
4. Is your personal website an advertising vehicle or a marketing vehicle, and why?
5. What is the value of joining your local CCIM chapter and regularly attending the meetings?

Chapter 11

Writing the Purchase Contract

120 Chapter 11

If you are representing a commercial buyer in a small- to mid-size-property acquisition, you will probably use your company's or your local real estate association's commercial purchase agreement, usually with an income property addendum of some sort. The important thing to recognize here is that you do not want to use a residential purchase contract for the purchase of income-producing property. The reason is clear: You are helping your client purchase more than just bricks and stone—you are helping your client to buy an income stream.

I don't know of a single residential purchase agreement that covers all the issues you need to address in the purchase of an income-producing property, and if you try to use that type of agreement, you will have to write in all the commercial issues by hand. The chances of your omitting something important are just too great, so don't do it.

The commercial purchase agreements that are available today have evolved over many, many years and are all-encompassing now. You will need to use language in the agreement that makes the purchase contingent on several issues to protect your buyer, some of which are as follows:

- Inspection and approval of the interior of all rental units are required.

- Inspection and approval of all leases and/or rental agreements, including any garage leases and washer/dryer leases, are also required.

- The agreement must be contingent on the inspection and approval of the seller's Schedule C from his/her personal 1040 tax returns, or of the equivalent form used for limited liability companies (LLCs) and corporations, and the accounting records showing all income/expense items for the past two years

Writing the Purchase Contract 121

(at a minimum), as well as the current year-to-date income and expenses incurred.

- There needs to be a provision for the buyer to receive Estoppel Certificates from all tenants prior to close of escrow. (This Certificate is not always required on large apartment complexes, but for proper due diligence it is best to include it in your purchase agreement.) I have found that all too often, real estate agents who present themselves as commercial specialists don't even know what an Estoppel Certificate is. It is a written statement signed by each tenant that states the tenant's name(s), the address and unit number of the premises the tenant occupies, the amount of rent the tenant is currently paying, the amount of any last month's rent and/or security deposit the current owner or property management company is holding on the tenant's behalf, and a statement that the tenant is not currently in bankruptcy proceedings or withholding rent from the owner for any reason (e.g., unsuitable living conditions).

Every one of these requirements is vitally important for your buyer to know about the property *before* he/she becomes the owner.

As an example, I represented an investor in a tax-deferred exchange in San Francisco whereby he was trading into a 10-unit apartment house at the base of Nob Hill. The owner and the resident manager both told us what the current rents were, and we made our calculations as to the value from there. They were visibly upset when my offer required Estoppel Certificates—and no

> Every one of these requirements is vitally important for your buyer to know about the property *before* he/she becomes the owner.

122 *Chapter 11*

wonder. I became suspicious while we were looking at the interior of the units. I asked several of the tenants what their rent was, and I told them they would be required to sign an affidavit to that effect. It then came out that they were paying the rent stated on the leases but were getting a cash kickback from the owner. He was trying to pump up the value of the building in this manner and would have been very happy to have my client inherit the whole mess. We made a requirement of getting new leases signed at the real rents and adjusted our offer accordingly. The tenants were actually relieved, the seller was so embarrassed that he went along with whatever we wanted, and the resident manager was fired.

Something that is not prewritten into many commercial purchase contracts is the written approval of the buyer's legal and/or tax counsel. *This is a must!* You must see that every single commercial contract that you draft on behalf of a client says, *"This sale is contingent on the express written approval of the buyer's tax and/or legal counsel within ten days after final acceptance of this offer."*

Sometimes your client will be totally satisfied with the transaction and won't go to an attorney or CPA. That's your client's choice; however, make sure that you give your client the right to do it as a contingency of the sale or exchange. Many attorneys don't like to give opinion letters, so I always include a "drop-dead" clause along with the previously cited contingency language that furthers that statement by saying, *"Any objections shall be made in writing within said ten days by the buyer's tax and/or legal counsel or this contingency shall be considered waived by the buyer."*

If your client is purchasing or selling property in the name of an LLC, trust, real estate investment trust (REIT), or other legally created entity, note right away that the title company will require a copy of the agreement with the LLC or REIT, or whatever the entity is, to see if it will issue a title insurance policy on the property. Some people will be reluctant to give the agreement to you, but

Writing the Purchase Contract 123

they must give it to the title company. Some clients like to make the offer in their own name "and/or assignee." This gives them the contractual right to assign the purchase to literally anyone during the escrow period. Arizona law says that real estate purchase contracts are assignable unless there is a specific clause to the contrary in the purchase contract, but the law in other states may be different, and you will need to be aware of the provisions in yours, as well as the provisions in the purchase contract.

NOTE: If you are the listing agent and a contract is presented to you that says "and/or assignee," you may want to counteroffer and make the buyer name any assignee within a short time instead of going the entire escrow period before you find out who the real purchaser is.

Be sure to give yourself sufficient time to conduct the escrow. Currently a 90-day minimum is prudent because you will want to be sure the client successfully negotiates any property condition issues before paying in advance for an expensive appraisal. The due diligence period is usually longer for income property than it is for a home purchase because there are more issues to investigate. The financing can also take longer to obtain because the lender may have many leases and the accounting records to review. If your client has a property to sell to a third-party purchaser to effect a tax-deferred exchange, you will most certainly want a longer escrow on the purchase leg of the transaction to allow sufficient time to market the property. You will also need to make the contract contingent on the sale of the buyer's property to a third-party purchaser within a certain number of days. That way, if you don't have the down-leg property sold in time to complete the exchange, you will not be in default on the contract and your client will not lose a deposit. If not already included, you should insert the clause *"This sale/exchange is contingent on the sale of the buyer's property at [address] to a third-party purchaser within [number of days] after final acceptance of this offer."*

124   *Chapter 11*

Finally, it is clearly in your client's best interest, if he/she is making a tax-deferred exchange, to have an "intent" clause in the contract. This should state, *"It is the sole intent of the buyer named herein to effect a tax-deferred exchange of the equity in the property commonly known as [address] for the equity in the property stated in line [number] of this contract. The seller agrees to cooperate with the buyer in said exchange, including the use of an intermediary, pursuant to IRC Section 1031 at no additional cost or liability to the seller."*

> It is clearly in your client's best interest, if he/she is making a tax-deferred exchange, to have an "intent" clause in the contract.

NOTE: Please remember, the scope of this book is not to discuss how to practice law but to give you a good working knowledge of how to conduct yourself as a successful commercial agent. Please review all references to contract language with your own attorney and broker prior to use.

When you are dealing in larger properties, where you often have a much more sophisticated buyer, it will be common for you to start the negotiations with a nonbinding letter of intent (LOI). A sample LOI is provided for you in Appendix 2, and its format can easily be duplicated in a Word file.

This letter, which your client will sign, is a nonbinding statement of all the major facts and issues under which your client will be willing to purchase a certain property. Once the LOI is signed by your client, you will get it to the listing agent by fax, in an email attachment, or in some other fashion. A word of caution here: If you fax, email, or otherwise send a contract or counteroffer to another agent, do not assume that it has gone through. Do two things: First, wait to see if the fax goes through or the email is kicked back to you without delivery; if you are quite sure the LOI has been

Writing the Purchase Contract **125**

delivered, call to notify the agent or leave a message to confirm that you have sent it. Some type of verbal exchange will have taken place between you and the listing agent prior to your sending the LOI. However, when you finally do send it to the agent, be sure to include a short letter with your client's qualifications and any other pertinent information that will be important to the seller. This initial negotiation is typical in the purchase of large tracts of land and other large properties.

Once the major terms have been worked out in this manner, your client will sometimes have his/her own attorney draft the actual purchase agreement. Your main function at this time is to communicate with the buyer's attorney to ensure that all the terms and conditions previously agreed to are incorporated in the final draft of the purchase agreement, and you should review it before sending it to the listing agent. Your commission will often be included as a condition of this type of purchase agreement, but be sure that there is a written statement somewhere that clearly spells out the total agent compensation, who is liable to pay it, and when and how it is split. Failure to see to this matter will almost always make you the recipient of a "commissionectomy."

> Failure to see to this matter will almost always make you the recipient of a "commissionectomy."

After you have drafted the purchase agreement and your buyers have signed it, give them a copy and ask them to review it carefully. Then, contact the listing agent, notify him/her of the offer, and ask how he/she would like to proceed. If possible, you should be there to present your buyers' offer in person; however, many owners do not live near their rental property, and the listing agent will need to send the offer to them electronically and discuss it with them over the phone. If this is true, you should send along with your contract a letter that tells a little about the buyers and what

126   *Chapter 11*

qualifications they have that will make this a successful transaction. If you cannot be there in person to present the offer, be sure to send along any comparable sales you have that make your case regarding the offered price.

If you get a counteroffer that includes a price increase, complete another Annual Property Operating Data (APOD) statement at the new price before you meet with your buyers. This way, they will be able to see what the counteroffer really means to them in terms of cash flow for the new property, and they will be better able to make an informed decision.

Review Questions

1. When representing clients in a commercial property purchase, what are you really helping them invest in?
   A. the physical property
   B. an income stream or potential value increase
   C. the pride of owning the property
   D. all of the answer choices

2. When is the only time a residential purchase agreement and income property addendum should be used?
   A. when making an offer to purchase four or fewer residential units
   B. any time, as long as the addendum is used
   C. never
   D. when it is what the investor prefers

Writing the Purchase Contract   127

3. Because contract deliverance is considered acceptance, what is the prudent thing to do after you email a signed, fully accepted counteroffer to the listing agent?

   A. wait a while to see that your email goes through and then call the listing agent to confirm receipt; leave a voicemail as well

   B. call the listing agent to say that you have sent him/her the signed counteroffer

   C. email the signed counteroffer to him/her and go home

   D. drive to the listing agent's office to drop off the hard-copy signed counteroffer

4. What is the most effective method of presenting a purchase agreement to a seller?

   A. fax or email it directly to the seller and let the listing agent know you have done so

   B. fax or email the offer to the listing agent

   C. fax or email the offer to both the listing agent and the seller simultaneously

   D. deliver the offer in person

5. You get a counteroffer that includes a price increase. What should you do before discussing it with your buyer?

   A. write down the important issues in the purchase contract and then call the buyer

   B. immediately call the buyer about the changes requested by the seller in the counteroffer

   C. fill out a new APOD before calling the buyer to discuss the changes requested

   D. fill out a new APOD and send it and the counteroffer to the buyer; then wait for him/her to call you

128　*Chapter 11*

Class Discussion Topics

1. Discuss the proper use of the correct purchase agreement.
2. What is an Estoppel Certificate, and when is it used?
3. When writing a purchase agreement for an office building, how many years of accounting records should you require, and why?
4. Discuss the importance of making a purchase agreement contingent on the written approval of the buyer's tax and/or legal counsel. Who are the individuals it protects, and how does it protect them?
5. When delivering a fully accepted offer or counteroffer to the cooperating agent, it is prudent to do what? Why?

Chapter 12

Conducting the Commercial Escrow

130   *Chapter 12*

There are, of course, two sides to every escrow: the seller's side and the buyer's side. Let's take each side and talk about the issues that must be addressed by the agent representing that side.

The Listing Agent or Seller's Representative

Once an agreement has been reached, escrow must be opened, or an appointment must be made with a closing attorney, just as for a residential transaction. The purchase contract will usually dictate who opens the escrow (and with whom) or who contacts the attorney.

Your job as the seller's agent is to see that escrow is opened in a timely manner and that any deposit referenced in the purchase agreement has been placed into escrow by the buyer's agent in a timely manner per the contract terms. Because earnest money deposits must be placed into a neutral depository (i.e., an escrow or broker's trust account) by the end of the following business day after an offer is accepted, if you haven't heard from the buyer's agent by late afternoon of the next business day, you need to call the agent to ask if escrow is opened. If not, probe as much as necessary to find out why. Is it a case of buyer's remorse or just a slow-moving agent? Stay on top of this because it is often a sure sign of pending trouble later in the escrow.

Get the escrow company's name, escrow agent's name, phone and fax numbers, and the escrow number. In the eastern area of the United States, where closing attorneys are employed in real estate transactions, get the full information about the closing attorney. Call to verify that the deposit has been placed into escrow or the closing attorney's trust account.

Conducting the Commercial Escrow 131

Create a timeline for the escrow, and get a copy to all parties to the escrow, including the escrow company or closing attorney. This timeline should outline the:

- dates each contingency must be waived by;

- dates any inspections must be ordered and/or conducted by; and

- escrow closing date and any other dates stated in the purchase contract.

Creating and using an escrow timeline is an excellent way to help conduct an orderly, efficient escrow.

As the seller's agent, you will need to obtain all leases and rental agreements, including parking agreements and washer/dryer rental contracts, from the seller. Photocopy them and get them to the buyer's agent for the buyer's review. You will also need to help the seller obtain Estoppel Certificates signed by all the existing tenants, and you will need to get the seller's Schedule C or limited liability company (LLC) equivalent from his/her federal income tax statement for the number of years dictated by the purchase contract. Schedule C shows the income derived from the seller's building and the operating expenses. Nearly all commercial purchase contracts have a clause in them that makes the contract contingent on the buyer's review and approval of these items. Buyers often want at least the last two years' operating statements to review. Obtain what the contract dictates, make photocopies, and get the copies to the buyer's agent as quickly as you can. Never give your copies to the cooperating agent; always keep the documents the owner gives you under your control.

Most commercial purchase agreements state that the sale is contingent on the buyer's written approval of the interior of all rental

132 Chapter 12

units or a sampling of the rental units. In large apartment complexes, this can be a difficult chore to coordinate, and care must be taken to adhere to the tenants' rights by way of giving proper and timely written notice of your intent to enter their apartment. The same practice applies to but is not as difficult with office buildings and is a little more difficult with medical buildings because of patient privacy issues. On large multifamily properties, it works well to arrange to have all rental units subject to a walk-through inspection by the inspector the investor has chosen and to name 15 to 20% to be available for a complete inspection. In units where the tenants are at home, ask them if there is anything that needs repairs or maintenance; it's within the scope of your due diligence to do that.

As soon as the preliminary title report or abstract of title is available, read it over very carefully. See that the names of the vested owners stated in the title report or abstract match the sellers' signatures on the purchase agreement, and carefully review the exceptions to title listed on Schedule B. If something doesn't look right, ask your broker, closing attorney, or your title company escrow officer about it. Schedule B of a title report shows exceptions to title; these include tax liens, real estate taxes not yet due and payable, liens and/or court judgments, and many other issues that could hinder the successful closing.

> As soon as the preliminary title report or abstract of title is available, read it over very carefully.

If the property is owned by a family trust, LLC, corporation, or other nonperson entity, obtain a copy of the trust agreement or corporate resolution and give it to the escrow agent or closing attorney. The closing attorney or title company legal department will want to read the agreement before issuing a title insurance

Conducting the Commercial Escrow   133

policy or giving an abstract of title to see that the person or persons required to sign the deed to be given to the new buyer have the legal authority to do so.

If the property is financed, obtain all the loan information from the sellers, including the lender's name, address, phone and fax information, and loan number, and give it to the escrow agent or closing attorney so that he/she can order any loan payoff demands when necessary.

Once these issues have been taken care of, your main job through the rest of the escrow is to keep the buyer and buyer's agent on track, help your sellers negotiate repairs requested by the buyers, and assist as you are able in helping the sellers clear any troublesome title and other such issues. An issue you will have to deal with sometimes is the death of a spouse. If the name of the deceased spouse still shows on the title report, you should assist the surviving spouse in getting the title officer a certified copy of the death certificate and in complying with any other requirement to clear the property's title.

Whether you are representing the buyer, the seller, or, especially, both parties, it is a *must* that you keep a complete communications log in your file or on your computer that lists every single thing you say and do during the entire escrow period. Every phone call, text, and email should be logged, along with a brief statement of what was said. Each activity you engage in should be noted, along with the date and time. An excellent piece of advice is to obtain a handheld digital tape recorder, and when you do or say something having to do with an escrow, tape a message about it. Once a week, take out or open your computer to all your escrow folders and play back and transcribe the noted activities into your communications log.

Why is this so important? If the escrow goes sideways and people start looking for someone to blame, they often have selective

134   *Chapter 12*

memory about things you told them, did for them, and so forth. In these instances, a good communications log is your very best friend.

An excellent piece of advice is to obtain a handheld digital tape recorder, and when you do or say something having to do with an escrow, tape a message about it.

Another point is to put everything in writing and convey it to whomever it must go to in such a fashion that you can prove you sent it or conveyed it. The best methods are as follows:

- If you email something to someone, blind-copy (BCC) yourself, print out the email, and put it in your escrow folder or save it to an online file you have created for that property.

- If you fax something to someone, be sure to staple the fax cover sheet showing the date and time of what you faxed, put it in your escrow folder, and enter it into your communications log or scan and save it to your digital file.

- If you hand-deliver something to someone, have an additional copy of whatever it is with you, and have the person sign "Received" and date it. Put it in your file and communications log. If the person will not sign it, write "(buyer/seller) would not sign for delivery."

The Selling Agent or Buyer's Representative

Most contracts dictate that the buyer selects the escrow agent, and so the buyer's agent usually opens the escrow. If this is the case,

Conducting the Commercial Escrow 135

you should open the escrow as soon as possible, but absolutely within the time prescribed by the contract or state law. Have all your buyers' full names and their complete contact information with you when you open the escrow, and give it to the escrow agent or closing attorney along with the earnest money deposit. In most states, the purchase agreement also acts as escrow instructions; if this is true in your state, be sure to give the escrow agent or attorney a copy of the purchase agreement and any counteroffers and addenda as well. Ask the escrow agent to call the other broker to notify him/her of the escrow number and all necessary escrow company phone and fax numbers. Have the escrow agent verify to the listing agent that you have given the escrow agent the deposit check.

If your buyer is financing the purchase and you know who the lender is, ask the escrow agent to see that a digital copy of the preliminary title report is delivered to the proper loan officer at the lending institution as soon as he/she receives it. You and the buyer should also obtain a digital copy sent to you as an email attachment. Read the report thoroughly! Check the owners' names referenced in the report against those given in the purchase agreement to verify that they match. If the property is owned by an LLC or corporation, ask the title representative to be sure to check for proper authority to sign on behalf of the LLC or corporation. Read Schedule B to see there are no exceptions to title that will adversely affect your client. Give a copy to your client and obtain written acknowledgment that he/she has received it, or ask your client to send you an email acknowledging he/she has received it. Usually a dated "Received" on another copy is sufficient.

Call the seller's agent to request copies of the leases, Estoppel Certificates, and accounting records specified in the purchase agreement. Remember to log all this into your communications log. Most sellers will not want to get Estoppel Certificates signed until all the buyers' contingencies are waived.

136   *Chapter 12*

> Call the seller's agent to request copies of the leases, Estoppel Certificates, and accounting records specified in the purchase agreement. Remember to log all this into your communications log.

Set a mutually acceptable date and time to see the inside of the rental units if the contract calls for doing so. Call your buyer to verify the date and time.

Give a copy of the purchase contract to the loan officer and ask if he/she has received the preliminary title report or abstract of title yet. Ask what income/expense documents, if any, are needed to process the loan, and then ask the seller's agent for them. Document this as well.

Once you have received the required income/expense documents from the seller, review them carefully, make notes of anything that looks odd or suspicious, and then call the seller's agent to clarify each item as necessary. Make notes of all this. Take the documents to your buyer or scan and email them to your buyer, and then review them with him/her. Get copies to the lender if required to do so.

During the due diligence period, you need to order any termite, property, roof, or other inspections or other reports mandated by the purchase contract, set a time to conduct them, and ask the seller's agent to notify the tenants if entry into any of their units is necessary. It is wise to always suggest a termite/pest inspection and a roof inspection when representing a buyer in the purchase of any improved real estate because these can be big-ticket repairs. If zoning or re-zoning is an issue or a contingency of the sale, you need to get on it with the proper government authorities and/or legal representatives immediately because these things can take considerable time. Be sure to document your activities in your escrow folder and keep your clients notified of each step you take.

Conducting the Commercial Escrow 137

In certain areas, you need to check for flood zones, earthquake safety zones, city or county special assessments, and other such matters. If you aren't sure of yourself, ask a seasoned commercial agent in your area or your escrow agent what to watch out for. This period in an escrow is when most issues occur that can lead to legal problems related to an agent's nonperformance, so be extra diligent.

> This period in an escrow is when most issues occur that can lead to legal problems related to an agent's nonperformance, so be extra diligent.

Once the due diligence period is over and everything is successfully negotiated or disclosed *in writing*, your buyer's new financing is approved, and all contingencies have been waived in writing, it is time to get the paperwork signed and close the escrow. You should always accompany your client, whether buyer or seller, to the escrow signing. Not only is doing so a professional standard you should meet, but it also prevents a "commissionectomy" from taking place while you aren't there.

You should arrive at the closing at least 15 to 30 minutes early and ask to review the closing papers. Have your calculator with you to check the prorations, especially rents, security deposits, last month's rents, homeowners association fees, if any, and real property taxes. If the escrow agent makes a mistake and debits your client when he/she should have had a credit, your client takes a double hit because he/she not only didn't receive the credit but got debited as well.

Call the seller's agent to make arrangements to pick up any keys and other items that are to be transferred to the buyer. Pick them up and deliver them to the buyer. It is a good idea to meet the

138   *Chapter 12*

buyer at his/her new property a day or two after closing just to check things out.

Within one or two days after escrow has closed, write your buyers or sellers a handwritten thank-you note, thanking them for allowing you the pleasure of representing them in selling, exchanging, or acquiring their new property.

Review Questions

1. When opening an escrow by phone, what should you get from the escrow company?
   A. company's name, agent's name, and escrow number
   B. agent's name, agent's cell phone number, and company address
   C. company's address, phone number, and fax number
   D. agent's name, company's address, and escrow closing date

2. What documents must you obtain from the seller of an LLC-owned multifamily property you are listing?
   A. last two years' accounting records
   B. year-to-date accounting records
   C. LLC operating agreement
   D. all of the answer choices

3. You just received the preliminary title report. You checked the seller's name and found that the husband's name is still on title even though he passed away several years ago. What action should you take?
   A. ask the surviving spouse if she has a certified copy of her husband's death certificate and offer to assist her in getting one if she doesn't
   B. tell the spouse to let the title officer know her husband is deceased
   C. tell the cooperating agent that you will need to extend escrow
   D. do nothing (The title company will find out about it themselves.)

Conducting the Commercial Escrow 139

4. You represented the buyer in his purchase of a small industrial property. He is financing 65% of the purchase and wants to purchase the property in the LLC he has created. What should you tell him?
   A. Lenders won't loan money to him if he is using an LLC.
   B. Lenders won't lend money to an LLC, so he will have to purchase it in his own name and deed it to his LLC after escrow closes.
   C. You checked with his lender, and that's not a problem.
   D. LLCs are not used with industrial property.

5. You represent the buyer of a property that is NNN-leased to McDonald's Restaurant Corporation, and you just received the 45-page lease the regional franchise owner has signed with the seller. What should you do?
   A. read the lease thoroughly, making notes of anything you question
   B. check the lease expiration date and, if necessary, investigate renewal with the listing agent and McDonald's
   C. send a copy of the lease to your buyer and tell him it is his responsibility to review it
   D. both A and B answer choices

Class Discussion Topics

1. You have a listing on a 120-unit multifamily complex. What documents must you obtain from the seller, and when is the best time to obtain them?
2. Discuss the importance of creating an escrow timeline for each transaction, and give the class a description of the issues that need to appear on it.
3. Your client's name is John Smith. He is a widower. You just got the title report, and Schedule B shows the title vested in the names of John Smith and Jacqueline Smith, as joint tenants with right of survival. There is an IRS tax lien for $14,982.00 and a court judgment for $6,800.00. Discuss what action you need to take.

140   *Chapter 12*

4. You just opened escrow for the sale of a $9 million self-storage facility you are representing the buyers in the purchase of. Discuss what activities you need carry out and when they should be done.

5. Discuss why it is important to clearly and consistently document all of your activities and communications during an escrow and how to best maintain the written records.

Chapter 13

Financing Commercial Real Estate

142   *Chapter 13*

Single-family homes, condominiums, and owner-occupied apartment houses of four or fewer units are readily financed by savings and loans, savings banks, and mortgage brokers. However, these lenders do not ordinarily finance commercial real estate. Multifamily properties of five or more rental units are considered commercial real estate.

Multifamily properties of five or more units and all other types of commercial real estate are usually financed by life insurance companies, commercial banks, mortgage bankers, and real estate investment trusts (REITs).

The *mortgage underwriting* of an income-producing property involves much more analysis than is required for a home loan.

Risk Aversion

Although the real estate serves as the collateral for the financing, it is not the primary defense against loss to the lender. No lender wants to obtain ownership of a property through foreclosure resulting from a borrower's default. The lender's first line of defense against having to foreclose on a property is to reduce the probability of the borrower's defaulting on the loan in the first place.

The most effective means of ensuring prompt and continuous payment of a loan on income-producing property is to accurately forecast the income flow from which the debt servicing will be paid. This is a fundamental underwriting tenet.

> The lender's first line of defense against having to foreclose on a property is to reduce the probability of the borrower's defaulting on the loan in the first place.

Debt Coverage Ratio

Most lenders that finance investment real estate projects are concerned more with the relationship between net operating income (NOI) and annual debt service (ADS) than they are with the loan-to-value ratio (LTV). The reason for this is the general lack of agreement concerning the property's value and/or the overall rate used to capitalize the NOI.

The foundation of the value of income-producing real estate is the future income stream. The key to estimating the future value of this income rests in estimates of the *amount, timing, duration,* and *stability* of future income flows. The process of converting these future income flows to a present value is a simple matter of capitalization at the appropriate rate. In the area of mortgage lending on income-producing property, the appropriate rate can sometimes present quite a problem, particularly when the overall rate of return on the property combines such factors as the tax situation of the typical investor, typical financing terms, appreciation, and length of ownership of the investment.

As indicated earlier, the lender is not interested in acquiring the property by default. That is always the *final* step in protecting the money that has been loaned. The *first* line of protection is the *income stream,* for it is from the income stream that the lender will be repaid. Loan payments include interest on the loan and periodic principal payments. Thus, the lender is much more concerned with a careful examination and analysis of the validity of estimates of NOI than it is with estimates of the property's current market value.

Lenders use a *debt coverage ratio* (DCR) to compare ADS with NOI. The DCR is the NOI divided by ADS.

$$DCR = \frac{NOI}{ADS}.$$

144 *Chapter 13*

The lender's margin of safety—that debt payments can be met by the property's income—increases as the coverage ratio increases.

Example of Debt Coverage Ratio

A loan that requires ADS of $96,000, with an NOI of $120,000, would have a coverage ratio of

$$\frac{\$120,000}{\$96,000} = 1.25.$$

In this case, NOI could decline 20% (from $120,000 to $96,000) before the lender would have to rely on the owner to contribute to debt service from other financial resources.

Based on experience, lenders may specify a maximum DCR for different types of property. In the case of an NOI that can be forecast with a high degree of accuracy with respect to size, duration, and timing, such as a long-term NNN lease with an AAA-rated tenant, the lender will usually require less margin between NOI and ADS, thereby giving a lower coverage ratio. Accordingly, an increased risk or uncertainty in the NOI will increase the DCR.

> Based on experience, lenders may specify a maximum DCR for different types of property.

Determination of Maximum Loan Amount

A lender will make a 7% loan with monthly payments for 30 years. The required DCR for the subject property by that lender is 1.25. NOI is $96,000. First determine the monthly payment:

Financing Commercial Real Estate 145

$$\frac{NOI}{DCR} = ADS.$$

$$\frac{\$96,000}{1.25} = \$76,800.$$

Monthly debt service (loan payments) are:

$$\frac{ADS}{12} = \frac{\$76,800}{1.25} = \$6,400 \text{ per month.}$$

The maximum loan on the subject property is the present value of an annuity (the loan payments) at 7% per year with monthly compounding for 30 years. The known values are as follows:

Payment = $6,400 per period (month).

Amortization period = 30 (years) × 12 = 360 periods.

Interest = 7%/12 = 0.58% per period.

You would put the following values in your calculator:

$6,400 = PMT.

360 = N.

0.58 = I.

$965,865 = PV (loan amount).

The maximum loan would probably be rounded to $966,000.

One of the first things an agent who is new to commercial real estate should do after getting settled is to ask for the names of several local or nearby lenders who finance commercial real

146 *Chapter 13*

estate. If you know any residential loan agents, ask them for referrals. Call the referred commercial loan agents and offer to buy them lunch. Remember, they are also looking for new sources of business as well and will usually be happy to meet with you.

While at lunch or at your meeting, ask the loan agents questions about how they work and get details about their firm's lending requirements. Here are some examples of questions to ask:

- What sort of commercial properties does your bank like to lend on the most?

- What type of property will your bank not lend on?

- What will you need from my client before you will start processing his loan?

- What is an average amount of time it takes for your bank to approve a loan?

- What is your bank's current LTV ratio?

- What is your bank's current debt-servicing ratio?

Most commercial banks and credit unions are not interested in financing industrial property because there are too many inherent risks associated with it. Pollution is the number 1 issue, especially if the pollution has entered the groundwater. If a lender makes a loan on an industrial property that at some point in time is cited for pollution issues and the buyer walks away, and then the lender forecloses on the property, they will be co-liable for the cost of the environmental cleanup, which can easily run into hundreds of thousands of dollars or more.

If you are going to specialize in industrial property, seek out an industrial specialist with either your company or another, and ask

Financing Commercial Real Estate **147**

the specialist for a referral to a lender that will finance industrial properties. An excellent way to meet industrial specialists is to join and attend the Certified Commercial Investment Member (CCIM) monthly luncheons in your area. Remember, self-storage properties are classified as industrial properties.

Review Questions

1. Which of the items below is most important to a lender?
   A. loan-to-value ratio
   B. debt coverage ratio
   C. capitalization rate
   D. net operating income

2. Which of the following is used to calculate net operating income (NOI)?
   A. gross operating income minus vacancy and credit loss
   B. gross scheduled income minus gross operating income
   C. gross operating income minus operating expenses
   D. gross scheduled income minus net operating income

3. Why would a lender reduce the required debt coverage ratio from 1.25 to 1.12%?
   A. The buyer has an excellent financial statement, and the property location is excellent.
   B. The buyer is an experienced operator of the property type for which he/she is requesting a loan
   C. The buyer's FICO score is 635.
   D. both A and B answer choices

4. How important is it for a commercial agent to establish a trusted banking connection?
   A. not at all important
   B. somewhat important
   C. important
   D. extremely important

148 *Chapter 13*

5. What do the initials DCR stand for?
   A. debt coverage rate
   B. debit coverage ratio
   C. debt coverage ratio
   D. none of the answer choices

Class Discussion Topics

1. Your 75-unit multifamily listing went under contract, and the buyer's agent opened escrow the same day. It is now three days later, and the escrow company just called you to say they still haven't received the buyer's earnest money deposit, which was due two days ago. What should you do?
2. What is the primary purpose for which a lender uses a DCR, and why?
3. Brandon is a first-time owner of a self-storage unit. What issues came into play in the lender's decision as to what DCR to use?
4. Why is it of paramount importance for you to immediately read the entire preliminary title report when you receive it?
5. Explain the difference between LTV and DCR.

Chapter 14

Managing Commercial Property

150   *Chapter 14*

Property management has become a highly specialized field, with some firms specializing in residential income properties while others exclusively manage retail shopping centers, office buildings, or some other type of commercial property.

Whereas owners of small commercial real estate investments often tend to manage their own properties, most owners of midsize-to-large commercial properties do not want to become involved with the day-to-day management of their commercial real estate investments; instead, they employ the services of a professional firm to oversee them. This is often advisable from a legal standpoint as well as an operational one. Many laws must be adhered to, such as the Americans with Disabilities Act (ADA) and fair housing issues. Serious commercial property owners usually want the added benefit of a professional manager handling compliance with these and other legal issues such as timely return of tenants' deposits and eviction proceedings.

> Serious commercial property owners usually want the added benefit of a professional manager handling compliance with these and other legal issues such as timely return of tenants' deposits and eviction proceedings.

The Institute of Real Estate Management (IREM) awards the professional designation of Accredited Management Organization (AMO) to a company that meets the following standards:

- at least one Certified Property Manager (CPM) in charge

- annual accreditation renewal

- adherence to minimum standards and the rules set by IREM

- property management as a primary activity

Many property management firms specialize only in condominium association management. These firms collect homeowners association dues, send newsletters, hold the required annual meetings, enforce sanctions against homeowners who violate rules, prepare tax returns, and handle workers' compensation and insurance claims. Virtually all property management firms work under a management agreement whereby the firm is empowered with specific duties and obligations on behalf of the property owner. The three types of property managers include the following:

- *licensed property manager.* This person is a licensed real estate agent employed by a real estate firm that manages property or an individual broker who manages property for others for a fee. Persons working under the direct supervision of a licensed property manager need not be licensed.

- *individual property manager.* This person manages a single property for an owner and may or may not be a real estate licensee. This is usually a salaried position and may or may not include free use or reduced rent of one of the building's rental units.

- *resident manager.* A resident manager lives on the premises and may be employed by the owner or a property management firm. This person usually has special training or previous experience and the type of personality that lends itself to dealing well with tenants. Some necessary traits include the following:

  - sales skills necessary to "show and sell" the rental units

  - computer and data analysis skills

  - ability to identify problematic maintenance issues and ensure proper and timely care of the property

  - take-charge attitude and a high degree of confidence

152 *Chapter 14*

- accuracy in handling bookkeeping duties, money, and bank deposits

- keen sense of what is happening on the premises and in the area

- ability to select residents on the basis of credit reports and personal references

- ability to make timely and accurate reports

State-Defined Responsibilities

A property manager who is licensed as a real estate professional must act in a fiduciary capacity as the agent of the owner. State licensing laws charge each property manager with a list of specific duties, which include the following:

- paying insurance premiums and taxes and recommending tax appeals when warranted

- establishing the rental schedule that will bring the highest yield consistent with good economics

- keeping abreast of economic and competitive market conditions

- merchandising the space and collecting the rents

- frequently inspecting vacant space

- creating and supervising maintenance schedules and repairs

Managing Commercial Property 153

- planning alterations and modernizing programs

- supervising all purchasing

- advertising and publicizing vacancies through selected media and broker lists

- developing a policy for landlord-tenant relations

- auditing and paying bills

- maintaining proper records and making regular reports to the owner

- hiring, instructing, and maintaining satisfactory personnel to staff the building(s)

- qualifying and investigating prospective tenants' credit

- preparing decorating specifications and securing estimates

- preparing and executing leases

> State licensing laws charge each property manager with a list of specific duties.

Specific Duties

Under a property management agreement, the manager assumes all executive functions of the owner and is fully in charge of the details connected with the operation and physical upkeep of the property.

154   *Chapter 14*

> Under a property management agreement, the manager assumes all executive functions of the owner.

A conscientious manager is responsible for the following:

- handling residents' questions promptly and properly

- never denying a resident's request without clearly stating why

- advising renters what is expected of them and what they can expect from the owner (this should be in writing as a matter of policy)

- treating residents fairly and sympathetically

- using care to protect the tenants' and prospective tenants' legal rights with regard to fair housing and ADA issues, among others.

Establishing Rent Schedules

The law of supply and demand in an area dictates the amount set for rents. To set proper rent schedules, the manager must make a thorough analysis of the neighborhood and immediate area. The analysis should include but not be limited to:

- current area vacancy factors

- availability of transportation, recreation, churches, and schools and proximity to shopping

Managing Commercial Property 155

- trends in population growth and occupants per unit

- character, age, and condition of the immediate neighborhood

- financial ability and size of families in the immediate area

- directional growth of the community and the economic health of local businesses

- condition of the housing market versus population growth trends

The objective of good property management is to achieve a level of rent and vacancy that provides the highest net return to the property owner. Conducting regular rental surveys and establishing competitive rent schedules is primary to this objective. Bad tenants who use and often abuse a property while not paying rent are worse than having a vacant unit. The only competition a vacant unit has is other vacant units, not rented units.

> The objective of good property management is to achieve a level of rent and vacancy that provides the highest net return to the property owner.

Proper Accounting Records

Although the number of bookkeeping records needed depends on the type of property managed and the volume of business involved, the selection and maintenance of an adequate trust account system are essential in property management because of the fiduciary nature of the business.

156   *Chapter 14*

The property management broker is charged with the responsibility of trust fund recordkeeping. An annual audit by an outside accounting firm is highly recommended.

The following are reasons for keeping accounting records:

- The law states that a separate record must be kept for each managed property.

- They provide the broker with a source of information when problems arise or an enquiry is made.

- They are necessary for income tax purposes.

- They serve as controls in analyzing costs, preparing budgets, and evaluating income and expenses.

- Contractual relations and the Business and Professions Code mandate a complete and accurate accounting of all funds.

- They are required for full disclosure and accounting to third parties with an interest in the property.

- The fiduciary relationship between the owner and the manager dictates full disclosure.

A property manager must be fully aware of both the landlord's and the tenants' responsibilities.

Tenant's Responsibilities

According to the civil code of most states, a tenant must:

- keep the living unit clean and sanitary

- use all utility fixtures properly

Managing Commercial Property 157

- use the property only for its intended lawful purpose

- pay rent on time

- dispose of garbage and other waste in a sanitary manner

- abide by all rules and regulations

- give a written 30-day notice when vacating

- return door and mailbox keys when vacating

- leave the unit in a clean condition when vacating

Landlord's Responsibilities

A residential lease has an implied warranty of habitability. This does not extend to issues caused by a lack of tenant cleanliness. The landlord must keep the property in reasonably good order, including the plumbing, heating, electrical systems, and all areas under the landlord's care. The roof must be kept free of leaks, and all health and safety issues (e.g., loose railings or open access to a swimming pool) should be addressed in a reasonable time frame.

If the landlord allows the property to fall into a state of *uninhabitable* disrepair or the property becomes uninhabitable because of health and safety issues, the landlord cannot collect any rent. Violating this may subject the landlord and/or the property manager to actual and special damages from the tenants. A tenant can also raise the defense of habitability against an eviction notice.

If a landlord fails to make a timely correction of a repair that is his/her responsibility, the tenant has three options:

158   *Chapter 14*

1. The tenant may abandon the property and not be held liable for back rents or an unfulfilled lease.

2. The tenant may refer the problem to a mediator, an arbitrator, or, for serious problems, small-claims court.

3. The tenant may notify the owner in writing of an emergency situation that must be taken care of. If the owner fails to respond, the tenant may call his/her own repair people and offset the repair costs with up to one month's rent on the next rent check. States impose a maximum number of times this may be used by a tenant in each year of tenancy, so check with your local and state authorities about this issue. In many states, a tenant cannot be prohibited from installing a satellite dish within the area under the tenant's control, so check with your local and state authorities about this issue as well.

Assignment versus Sublease

A tenant has the right to assign or sublease his/her interest in a property unless the lease specifically prohibits it.

An assignment transfers the entire leasehold rights to a third party. The third party pays his/her rent directly to the original lessor, and the original lessee is eliminated.

A sublease of property transfers only a part of a tenant's interest. The sublessee pays his/her rent to the original lessee, who in turn is still responsible for payment of rent to the lessor. The original lessee has what is referred to as a "sandwich lease."

A lease should clearly indicate whether it may be assigned or subleased. Leases often state that no subletting or assignment shall take place without the express written permission of the lessor, which shall not be unreasonably withheld.

Termination of a Lease

A tenancy for a specified period, such as an estate for years, requires no notice of termination because the date has already been specified. A month-to-month tenancy necessitates a written 30-day notice because of its perpetual existence. It is always a good idea for a tenant to give a landlord a written notice in any event.

Evictions and Unlawful Detainer Actions

A landlord may evict a tenant and bring an unlawful detainer action against the tenant for failure to pay rent when due, violations of provisions contained in the lease or rental agreement, or failure to vacate the premises after termination of 30 days' written notice. Removing a tenant for nonpayment of rent entails the following process:

1. The landlord serves the tenant with a three-day notice to pay or quit the premises.

2. If the tenant fails to heed the notice, the landlord files an unlawful detainer action in municipal court.

3. If the landlord wins, the court awards the landlord a judgment. The landlord then asks for a writ of possession authorizing the sheriff to evict the tenant.

4. The sheriff sends the tenant an eviction notice. If the tenant fails to leave, the sheriff then physically removes the tenant.

160   *Chapter 14*

Many state legislatures have authorized city attorneys and prosecutor offices to bring unlawful detainer actions to abate drug-related nuisances. The landlord is charged fees and costs.

If a small-claims court action is necessary to recoup money from a tenant for lost rent or property damage, an owner or property manager may do so without the aid of an attorney. The maximum amount is the amount set by the small-claims court.

Retaliatory Eviction

In some states, a landlord cannot decrease services, increase rent, or evict a tenant within 180 days after the tenant exercises a right protected under the law, including:

- lawfully organizing a tenant association;

- complaining to a landlord about the habitability of the premises; or

- complaining to a public agency about property defects.

A tenant cannot waive his/her rights against retaliatory eviction.

Prohibition of retaliatory eviction is a defense against eviction. If a landlord has been shown to have acted maliciously, the tenant is entitled to actual damages and punitive damages as set by local or state law.

Managing Commercial Property 161

Review Questions

1. The initials CPM stand for which of the following?
   A. College Professor in Management
   B. Controller of Property Managed
   C. Certified Paperwork Manager
   D. Certified Property Manager

2. Which of the following is a good trait for a resident manager to have?
   A. show and sell skills
   B. computer skills
   C. ability to identify probable maintenance issues
   D. all of the answer choices

3. Which of the following is a true statement?
   A. At least 30 days prior to termination of a one-year lease, the tenant must give the owner a written notice of intent to vacate.
   B. A month-to-month tenant must give the owner or manager a written notice of intent to vacate at least 90 days prior to vacating.
   C. In a five-year commercial lease, the tenant must give the owner or manager at least six months' notice of intent to vacate.
   D. A tenant on a one-year lease is not required to give a written notice of intent to vacate because the date has already been established.

4. Under a retaliatory eviction law, a tenant cannot be evicted for which of the following?
   A. lawfully organizing a tenants' association
   B. complaining about clothes left in the laundry room
   C. complaining about the manager increasing the service costs without permission
   D. all of the answer choices

162   *Chapter 14*

5. What is the first step an owner or manager must take if a tenant fails to pay rent?
    A. tender a Three-Day Notice to Pay or Quit
    B. file an unlawful detainer action against the tenant
    C. file a suit in small-claims court for the back rent and punitive damages
    D. none of the answer choices

Class Discussion Topics

1. What are the reasons an owner of commercial real estate hires a professional property manager?
2. Discuss the duties of an off-site property manager and why they are important.
3. Discuss the issues that need to be evaluated when establishing rent schedules and why they are important.
4. What are the seven reasons for keeping accounting records, and why are they important?
5. Peter and Mary Chan live in a rental home. The roof started leaking, and they contacted the owner, who self-manages the home, about it. It has been raining, and three weeks have gone by without any action by the owner. What options are available to the Chans?

Chapter 15

Commercial Leasing

164   *Chapter 15*

A primary responsibility of a property manager is leasing property or acting as a consultant in the drafting of a lease. While most property management firms also draft leases on behalf of the owners whose properties are under their care, some property management firms rely on companies that specialize in leasing property only, and they do not get involved with any other part of property management. This type of arrangement is usually limited to large portfolio-sized holdings that call for highly specialized knowledge of certain types of leases, such as very large high-rise office buildings with long-term leases, major tenants such as large grocery store chains that anchor many neighborhood shopping centers, big-box tenants such as Target and Petco, and the major tenants in regional malls such as J.C. Penny, Sears, and Dillard's. These leases usually run from 30 to 50 pages and are drafted by attorneys.

When a lease is created, the owner is the *lessor* and the tenant is the *lessee*. A leasehold estate arises when an owner or a property manager acting as the owner's agent grants a tenant the right to occupy the owner's property for a specified period of time for a valuable consideration.

Antidiscrimination

Rigid antidiscrimination issues must be dealt with properly. However, a leasing agent can discriminate against a tenant for legitimate reasons such as bad credit, late rent payments at a prior rental, noted property damage, or bankruptcy. When conducting leasing activities on behalf of nonresidential properties such as office buildings, restaurants, and self-storage facilities, the leasing

---

In Chapter 17 you will read a full interview I had with Bruce Suppes, who is highly esteemed by the entire southern Arizona commercial real estate brokerage community as the very best office leasing specialist in southern Arizona. His knowledge of the processes of obtaining and servicing listings, as well as leasing office space, will amaze you. His contact information is in Chapter 17, and he welcomes calls and emails.

agent must be very careful not to violate the Americans with Disabilities Act (ADA).

> Rigid antidiscrimination issues must be dealt with properly.

Leasing agents are under no obligation to accept a bad tenant; it is easier to turn these people down than it is to evict them. Leasing agents often charge a nonrefundable screening fee, and the amount that may be charged is usually set by state law. This fee is to cover the cost of gathering information about a prospective tenant to make a decision about renting to him/her.

The method of screening prospective tenants must be uniform in nature if the leasing agent is to avoid being charged with discriminatory rental screening practices.

> The method of screening prospective tenants must be uniform in nature if the leasing agent is to avoid being charged with discriminatory rental screening practices.

Lease Provisions

Although in some states leases for less than one year may be verbal, a good leasing agent will get *all* leases in writing, including short-term vacation property rental leases. A written lease has the effect of putting all the agreed-on terms and conditions in writing for the mutual protection of all parties, including the brokers. If leasing a property that is subject to rules and regulations, attach them as an addendum to the lease and have the tenant sign for them; also see that they are added by reference in the lease agreement.

166   Chapter 15

Don't try to draft a lease or use a cut-and-paste method of assembling a lease, because doing so may create errors and omissions that would probably be considered the unlawful practice of law. It is best to use the forms available through your local multiple listing service (MLS) for simple leases and month-to-month rental agreements and obtain the services of a real estate attorney for more complex leases, especially those of a commercial nature.

Names of the Parties

A lease must contain the full names of all parties. A lease to a party who is under the age of 18 requires an adult cosigner unless the underage party can prove he/she is an *emancipated minor* by reason of marriage or court order. It would be best to check with your attorney with regard to this matter. The parties must sign the lease "*jointly and severally,*" so that each party to the lease is liable for the entire rent, and you can look to one or all of the tenants for payment.

Dates

The lease must have a beginning and an ending date.

Description of the Premises

The demised premises must be described in such a way that there is no ambiguity. If a storage room, garage, or parking space is included, it should be clearly stated in writing. A lease for office space should state the approximate square footage and the unit number if possible.

Rent and Late Charge

The amount of rent and where and when it is due must be clearly stated. A provision must be made for a late charge if the rent is not received by a specified time on or after its due date. The late charge should not exceed the amount (usually expressed as a percentage of the rent) mandated by the laws of your state to avoid having it deemed too high and declared as an unenforceable penalty.

Waterbeds

Common waterbed agreements require the tenant to pay for a policy of waterbed insurance and use a waterbed liner.

Pets

Pet agreements are common in residential leases. They usually restrict the size and/or number of pets. A higher cleaning fee is usually charged to tenants with pets. States vary on whether these are refundable or not, so be sure to check with your broker or manager.

Inspection of the Premises

Some leases provide for pretenancy and end-of-tenancy walk-through inspections. Deficiencies must be noted on a form provided for this purpose, which must be signed by the tenant and the landlord or property manager. This is an excellent practice because it clearly serves as a basis for evaluating claims made at a later date.

168   *Chapter 15*

Cleaning and Security Deposits

A security deposit functions as an insurance policy for the landlord in the event the premises are left damaged or dirty or if rent is owed. Whereas nonrefundable *cleaning deposits* are not allowed in many states, a landlord may charge a security deposit in an amount set by the laws of each state. For instance, in California, a security deposit equal to two months' rent may be charged for an unfurnished unit and up to three months' rent for a furnished unit.

When the tenant vacates, the landlord is allowed to retain only as much of the tenant's deposit as is reasonably necessary to remedy tenant defaults. Any unused portion of the deposit must be returned to the tenant at his/her last known address within three weeks after the premises are vacated. Again, check your state laws regarding this time limit because it may vary. Failure of the landlord to comply with this statute may make him/her liable to the tenant through a small-claims-court action, an attorney, or a complaint filed by the tenant through the Consumer Protection Bureau.

Exculpatory Clause

Leases nearly always contain an exculpatory clause (i.e., hold-harmless clause) whereby the tenant relieves the landlord of any and all liability for personal injury or property damage that results from the owner's negligence or the condition of the property. These clauses are usually invalid in residential leases, even if the tenant has agreed to one of them, and his/her legal rights are still intact.

Right of Entry

Most leases contain a provision that allows the landlord to enter the premises for specific purposes. If a lease is lacking such a provision, the landlord can enter only when:

Commercial Leasing 169

- an emergency requires entry;

- the tenant consents to an entry;

- the tenant has surrendered or abandoned the premises;

- the landlord has obtained a court order permitting entry; or

- the entry is during normal business hours after reasonable notice (this time will vary by state) to make necessary or agreed-on repairs, alterations, or improvements or to show the premises to prospective or actual purchasers, mortgagees, tenants, workers, or contractors.

Proper Client Representation

When you represent a property owner, ask him/her for a copy of the lease he/she normally uses. Read it thoroughly and make a list of questions about anything that you don't fully understand, or that makes you uncomfortable, or that you know to be a violation of state or federal law. Meet with the owner to review your list, recommending changes, additions, or deletions you think appropriate. An owner of a nonresidential commercial property will nearly always use a lease agreement that has been drafted by an attorney. It will be your responsibility as the owner's representative to read the entire lease and ensure that when negotiations are finalized between the owner and a new tenant, the owner's interests have been seen to. You must also ensure that before signing the lease the tenant entered nothing into it that would be detrimental to the owner's interests. If tenant improvements are negotiated, stay in close contact with the owner and the agent representing the tenant and let them know of the progress made. A few days before the tenant's occupancy, have everyone meet at the premises for a final walk-through inspection to see that all agreed-on changes have been made properly and that there are no outstanding issues

170   *Chapter 15*

to be resolved. Note any deficiencies and immediately engage the proper contractor to remedy them.

When you represent a tenant, ask as many questions as necessary to discover the tenant's needs. Ask about the minimum and maximum number of square feet needed; any preferred locations or areas, as well as any to avoid; how much rent the tenant is comfortable paying; parking requirements, including the need for covered parking or not; whether the tenant prefers a ground-floor unit or one higher up; and so on. As soon as you have established a relationship with the tenant, tell him/her to provide the property owner with his/her personal and business financial statements. Many tenants today want to lease space in the name of a limited liability company they have formed. Most owners will let them do this; however, they will almost always insist on a personal guarantee by the tenant.

You will almost always start the negotiations on behalf of your tenant-client by drafting a nonbinding letter of intent (LOI). (A sample LOI is provided in Appendix 2.) It should spell out the parties to the agreement; the tenant's desired lease term, either in months or years; the amount of rent offered; any tenant improvements requested by the tenant; and any other major facts that are subject to negotiation. Draft the LOI, send or give it to your client, and ask that he/she read it carefully to see that all major needs or wants have been covered; if your client approves of the draft, have him/her sign it. Send the signed draft to the listing agent and follow up with a phone call to tell the agent that you have just sent him/her an LOI to lease the listing. Ask the agent to review it with the owner or manager and get back to you at his/her earliest convenience. It is important to remember that the desired outcome of these negotiations is a mutually acceptable lease agreement; it is not about who won and who lost, so be business cordial at all times. The owner will either accept the terms of your LOI or will want changes. Changes often come in the form of a return copy of your LOI that has been "redlined," which is a term used for a counteroffer. If you receive a redlined LOI, provide your client with a copy and discuss the requested changes with him/her. This offer-counteroffer process continues until an agreement is reached. At that time the listing agent will see that the actual lease agreement is drawn and send you a copy for your client to sign and return along with a deposit. It is of paramount importance that you read the entire lease agreement prior to your client's signing it! As an example of why this is so important, I represented a lady who owned a commercial interior design business. She wanted about 1,700 square feet in a business park. I found her a unit that she was happy with, and drafted the LOI. It was approved, and the lease was drafted and sent to me. It was supposed to be a modified gross lease where she was liable for the rent, janitorial, utilities, and any increase in the property taxes after the first year. What came back was an NNN lease whereby she would have been responsible for *all costs* incurred in the operation of the building; all taxes, insurance, interior and exterior maintenance, everything! I called the listing agent, and "nicely" told him of the mistake, and the new lease was executed.

> It is of paramount importance that you read the entire lease agreement prior to your client's signing it!

Types of Leases

Full-Service Lease, or Gross Lease

A full-service lease calls for the tenant to pay only the rent and nothing else. The owner pays for the property taxes, insurance, all maintenance, utilities, management, and any other expenses incurred in the operation of his/her property. The rent for this type

172   *Chapter 15*

of lease is usually somewhat higher than for other types of leases that share expenses in some fashion.

Modified Gross Lease

A modified gross lease calls for tenants to pay for the rent, usually their interior janitorial services, their utilities, and very often, in multiple-tenant properties, their percentage share of any increase in the property taxes and insurance for the property. If, for example, the space leased by your client is 12% of the total leasable space in the property, your client would be liable for 12% of any increase in the total property taxes and property insurance in the second year of the lease and every year thereafter. Some modified gross leases do not include the tax and insurance escalation clause.

Triple-Net Lease

Often referred to as an NNN lease, a triple-NET lease calls for the tenants to pay the rent and their percentage of virtually all operating expenses paid in conjunction with the operation of the property. Most often the owner pays these expenses and gives a detailed itemization to each tenant early in the following lease year that sets the amount of NNN charges the tenant will pay each month of the new year. This is calculated each year.

Annual Rent Escalation Clause

Commercial leases initially run for a period of from three to five years and may or may not have built-in rights to renew; however, leases for big-block retailers and major tenants are usually for as long as 20 years, with options to renew. Because commercial property leases are long in duration, they always contain a lease escalation clause stipulating that the base rent will automatically increase by a percentage of the then existing lease amount each year—most often 3%. The annual Consumer Price Index (CPI) method of increasing rents is rarely used as it is too cumbersome to calculate and varies from area to area.

Review Questions

1. Which statement is NOT true?
   A. Big-box stores always use the real estate association commercial lease.
   B. Most commercial leases for major tenants are drafted by the listing agent.
   C. Most commercial leases are more than 40 pages in length.
   D. both A and B answer choices

2. A leasing agent may discriminate against a prospective tenant for all the following reasons EXCEPT:
   A. the person's race or ethnicity
   B. a bad credit history
   C. a documented history of property damage
   D. a recent bankruptcy

3. What common terms for "tenant" and "landlord" are used in commercial leases?
   A. lessee and lessor
   B. renter and landlord
   C. tenant and owner
   D. lessor and landlord

4. Lease negotiations nearly always start with which step?
   A. A lease, signed by the prospective tenant, is sent to the listing agent.
   B. A nonbinding LOI is sent to the listing agent by the tenant's representative.
   C. The listing agent sends a lease to the tenant's representative to fill out and return.
   D. A binding LOI is sent to the landlord's representative.

174 *Chapter 15*

5. In an NNN-leased property, the lessee is liable for which of the following expenses?
   A. rent and personal-space utilities only
   B. his/her share of all expenses incurred in the operation of the property
   C. rent, personal-space utilities, and common-space maintenance only
   D. rent only

Class Discussion Topics

1. A lady comes to see you and says she needs new office space, but she must take possession within the next week. You question her about the urgency, and she comes clean that she has been evicted. What should you do?
2. The large multifamily complex you manage does not have a written rule about waterbeds. A prospective tenant says he has a water bed and wants to lease an upstairs unit. What action should you take? Will you use any lease addenda, and if so, why?
3. A client has just agreed to let you manage and lease his nine-story office building. Why is it a good practice to ask a new client for a copy of the lease he/she uses? What action should you take upon receipt of the lease?
4. A lady referred to you wants about 1,200 square feet of office or retail space with good visibility and near an assisted-living center. She can afford only about $1,200 a month. You know of a neighborhood retail center in an adult community that has been half empty for years; it would be a good fit for her if you can negotiate the rent from $15 per square foot to $7 per square foot. What action would you take?
5. Explain the difference between a gross lease and an NNN lease, and then tell the class which type of property would likely use each one.

Chapter 16

Success Patterns of High-Producing Commercial Agents

176 *Chapter 16*

In this chapter, several highly successful commercial agents I know personally share their three or four best tips for succeeding in commercial real estate. I asked them, "If a new agent or an experienced residential agent came to you and said they were going into commercial real estate, what advice would you give them?" Most interesting, you will find their responses both very diverse and much the same.

Here are their answers.

Bruce Suppes

Vice President, CBRE Commercial Brokerage
14 years' experience as an office specialist
Named a CoStar Power Broker for 10 straight years

1. Pick a specialty (office, industrial, retail, investment, etc.) and stay with it. "There are riches in niches." Every moment spent outside your specialty is one less moment spent within it.

2. Constantly read about your profession, your industry, and anything for that matter. Our clients deserve a professional who continues to improve their craft and strives to be the very best.

3. Attitude is everything, well, almost everything. Bring a great one every day, even if others don't, and make your meetings with clients, especially the first meeting, as memorable for them as possible.

4. Be ETBW (easy to do business with). Have fun! If you're not having fun, I guarantee you nobody else around you is either. Providing info and data is easy, delivering it in a professional yet entertaining, fun manner is quite another.

5. Commercial real estate is still sales, but in a commercial real estate world. It is, and always will be, about relationships. People buy from someone they like and trust. Continually ask yourself the question, "Would you buy from you?"

6. Follow-up is huge! Why even start the process if you aren't going to finish it? Whenever possible, return phone calls the same day. Don't ever assume who is a good prospect and who is not. You never know. After all, everyone is a potential client, or knows someone who is!

Pete Peterson

CEO/Partner, Stratton Group of
Keller Williams Southern Arizona
15 years' experience
Co-owner of 10 Expansion Partners in five states

1. Get a mentor *and* a coach. One to help you work in your business, navigate commercial transactions, and get advice and perspective from, and the other to help you work *on* your business as you will need to implement a lead-generation model, a budget model, an economic model, and an organization model. You are going to pay for education in business, either from lost transactions or through mentorship and coaching.

2. Look into joining a team to leverage someone who has already built and invested in the above-mentioned models.

3. Mastermind with others, and read. Success leaves clues, *and so do failures*. There are few new ideas, just better execution. Learn from others who have gone before you.

178   *Chapter 16*

4. Invest in real estate yourself. You are in the business of helping people build wealth through real estate ownership. Take your own advice.

Harvey Mordka

Broker/owner of Harvey Mordka Realty,
Tucson, Arizona
46 years' experience

1. Master your fear and trepidation.

"Fear of the unknown has kept many a person from pursuing an area of interest. Everyone seems to know and be pretty comfortable with the residential side of the business. Commercial seems to hold a fascination of bigger-ticket sales but comes with higher risk and higher potential liability. If you genuinely have an interest in doing commercial sales or leasing, then you need to set your fears aside and go on to tips 2 through 4."

> "If you genuinely have an interest in doing commercial sales or leasing, then you need to set your fears aside."

2. Educate yourself.

"Many people have a desire to do things but don't want to pay the price of educating themselves in the commercial arena. It's a commitment of time and money."

3. Make a commitment to success.

"Once you have eliminated the fear and have obtained the education, you are ready to commit to the daily activities of being successful. Technology has come a long way, but there is still the value of personalization. Seeing the people eyeball to eyeball and building personal relationships is invaluable to being successful. Your commitment to serving the buyers' and sellers' needs will reward you financially and with repeat and referral business in the future."

4. Do not be afraid to specialize.

"Each of us has a niche that we are comfortable in. Find what and where you are happiest and pursue that area. Do not be afraid to take risks and learn new territory to travel. We are blessed to live in a country that is only 230 years old. Look how far we have come as a nation. From a landing on the East Coast, being hunters and gatherers, farming, manufacturing, inventing, developing, railroads, airplanes, cars, arts/theater, sports venues, rural and urban parks, and more! Under all is the land! What share of the commercial market would you like?"

Gary Best, CCIM

Associate Broker with Realty Executives Southern Arizona
Former president of the Tucson Association of REALTORS®
47 years' experience

"OK, Bob, here goes: The single most important characteristic of success in commercial real estate and actually in any endeavor where high achievement is possible is *commitment,* far and away more than any other characteristic. I am reminded of two top world-class athletes: seven-time Tour de France Champion Lance Armstrong and Kerri Strug, from Tucson, who won Olympic gold for her and her team in the 1996 Olympics. Both have acknowledged pain in their journeys, probably more than they

180 *Chapter 16*

> "The single most important characteristic of success in commercial real estate and actually in any endeavor where high achievement is possible is *commitment.*"

acknowledged, but the strength of their commitment to doing the very best they could do is what sustained their efforts, especially at the very last moments of their respective competitions.

"The mastery of certain processes also goes a long way toward success, particularly in commercial real estate. Different words can be used and presented differently in various businesses, but these processes are, not necessarily in order of importance:

• thinking creatively

• communicating effectively

• organizing one's selling efforts

• management of time

• ability to overcome objections

• staying motivated

"Much has been written about these skills as applied to any goal-oriented environment, but they are critical. The application of these skills, while never perfect, will determine the level of success any person or group of people will be able to achieve. The *commitment* must be strong, as the adversity to achievement of worthy goals will certainly be strong. As I considered your question, I kept coming back to these basics again and again."

Maureen Vosburgh

Coldwell Banker Residential Brokerage
32 years' experience

"I joined an independent commercial firm in Hartford, Connecticut, when I first started in the mid-1980s. I was told I shouldn't plan on any closed transactions for at least two years. As fate would have it, by the end of my first year in the business I was responsible for the largest commercial sale ($28,500,000) in the company's history and became the number 1 agent in the entire company. I did it despite the fact that I was one of only two women in a company that was dominated by over 20 men and tremendous sexism. The general market was 'good old boy' through and through.

"Why was I successful?

- I listened to my clients and really focused on their needs.

- I cultivated my very first client, who, with his two partners, bought a small historic building from me. The same threesome joined with seven partners in two other firms to form a still-larger company. It was that group that bought the historic office building for $28,500,000.

- I communicated well with all of my clients (especially those 10). I kept in constant touch.

- I had many more commercial transactions, including several more with the original 'cast of 10,' and I remain close friends with my original contact, who now lives in Maine."

182   *Chapter 16*

Debbie Green

Long Realty Company
29 years' experience
Specializes in land brokerage

"Bob, as you know, I specialize in land brokerage, so my comments
are confined to that area. A good agent needs to look past the obvious, so here are the [four] top things an agent should look for
when representing someone in a land transaction:

- identify zoning in writing from the proper municipalities—
  and record the name of the person you talked to

- look for any deed recorded restrictions that could alter the
  zoning

- ask questions of the sellers like if they have ever been involved
  in or know of any legal judgments, claims, liens, and so forth,
  that have occurred that may alter the use by the next owner

- ask if they have any knowledge of the land being involved in a
  subdivision into five or less parcels, and research this yourself
  to verify (Leave a paper trail.)

Success Patterns of High-Producing Commercial Agents **183**

Review Questions

1. What is the one theme that seems to run through nearly all the interviews?
   A. Diversity of product is best because you don't miss any deals.
   B. It is best to specialize in several types of commercial real estate because if sales are slow in one, the others will keep you going.
   C. It is best to specialize in only one product type and to go "narrow and deep."
   D. It is best to specialize in two property types for needed diversity.

2. According to Bruce Suppes, ETBW means what?
   A. entertaining, tactful, bearable, and wise
   B. enlightened, timely, bountiful, and wishful
   C. easy to do business with
   D. energetic, tactful, busy, and wary

3. What models does Pete Peterson feel that your business should have?
   A. lead generation model and budget model
   B. contract model and budget model
   C. economic model and organizational model
   D. both A and C answer choices

4. According to Harvey Mordka, what problems are more prevalent in commercial real estate than in residential real estate?
   A. higher risk
   B. higher potential liability
   C. more demanding clients
   D. both A and B answer choices

184   *Chapter 16*

5. Maureen Vosburgh believes in constant contact with her clients. Her efforts culminated in how large a sale?
   A. $12,700,000
   B. $19,750,000
   C. $28,500,000
   D. $22,950,000

Class Discussion Topics

1. Why does Bruce Suppes think there are "riches in niches"?
2. Discuss the advantages and disadvantages of being a member of a real estate team.
3. Pete Peterson is a strong advocate of masterminding meetings with his peers. What is the advantage of this, and how would you implement it?
4. Discuss the importance of overcoming fear through education when you start a commercial real estate career, and identify some of the sources of that education.
5. Discuss what it is about land brokerage that makes it so prone to disputes and legal action.

Chapter 17

Conversations with Three Veteran Commercial Brokers

186   *Chapter 17*

Bob Herd's questions and comments are in **bold and italicized** print. Bruce Suppes', Pete Peterson's, and Paul Lindsey's comments are in regular print.

Bruce Suppes

Vice President, CBRE Commercial Brokerage
(520) 323-5155
bruce.suppes@cbre.com

Bruce, please tell our readers what brought you into real estate, and how and when you started.

It happened quite by accident. Someone I worked with at a prior employer/partner told me to talk to this guy who has been in commercial real estate for years. Being someone who had sold a tangible product or service their entire career, it was difficult to put my head around what was involved with real estate brokerage. So glad I found out!

If I remember correctly, you have had at least 50 lease or sale transactions a year for your entire 14-year career, conducted over 750 sale or lease transactions totaling nearly $200 million in volume, assisted in the lease or sale of over 2.2 million square feet of office space here in Tucson, and have been named a CoStar Power Broker every year since 2007—is that right?

Yes, it does pay to learn your craft well!

Tell me what or who directed you into retail and office leasing.

That decision was made for me by the designated broker, and I certainly didn't know the difference. Office properties were the greatest need at this real estate firm at the time, so they put me in there. I didn't know the difference at the time, but I am very thankful office properties are the specialty I pursued. Helping smart, business-oriented, professional people with their real estate needs is what I truly enjoy!

> The same thing happened to me when I joined Marcus & Millichap Commercial Brokerage. I was assigned to retail brokerage and enjoyed every minute of it, especially the huge support system.

Have you always been with CBRE, or did you start somewhere else?

CBRE is the only firm I've ever been with, and where I began my 14-year real estate career.

You are someone who has gained an excellent reputation for your knowledge and skills in office leasing. Do you see an advantage in the "narrow and deep" philosophy, where you specialize in only one particular sector of commercial real estate and become so knowledgeable about it that you excel at it versus doing many types of commercial brokerage?

I am a huge believer in the "narrow and deep" philosophy and becoming an expert in your field. Clients look to us for our expertise, and that can only be accomplished by focusing on a specific area or specialty. Any time spent outside our specialty is less time spent within it. I am busy all day long focusing only on office product, and don't have time for anything else anyway.

Are you part of a team, or do you work alone?

I work alone some of the time, and split the listings I get with a couple of different agents, both of whom are far more detail oriented than I am. My skills lie with being a hunter and finding

188   *Chapter 17*

new business, negotiating, and creating relationships out in the marketplace. My partners offer skills that are not my strength but are equally important in the process. They do more of the legal wordsmithing and being a lease technician offering expertise in the required back-end work. Together we bring a much broader group of skills and services to the client that are needed to get the transaction done.

> I can personally verify that! The last lease I did where I represented the tenant would have never come together if you were not the neighborhood retail center's representative. That took some real skill!

Bruce, do you have an assistant, or is the CBRE office staff all the support you need?

The office staff provides great support, and they are all I need. I do go back and forth on whether or not to hire an assistant so I can take on more business. It's a constant struggle, with each way of working, with each having its own set of advantages and disadvantages.

What is a typical day like for you?

I have my day planned out from the night before. I typically have at least one appointment and a couple of property tours scheduled. Gaps are filled in with time allocated for follow-up calls or prospecting. Calls for tours the same day arise, which can change things around a bit, so I do my best to have my administrative duties done before 9 a.m. or after 5 p.m.

Do you have a preference as to who you represent, lessors or lessees, or do you just take both as the opportunity arises?

Conversations with Three Veteran Commercial Brokers 189

I take both as they arise and will accept the assignment only if I truly believe I can allocate an appropriate level of time, energy, and service to the client.

Do you still prospect for new listings? If so, tell us a little about how you do it. Do you cold-call, call past clients, send mailings to owners, or something else?

I haven't prospected for listings for quite some time, only because I have a large client base of property owners who call me when there are vacancies in their center or building. I do prospect for tenant or buyer clients via networking events. If there is a larger tenant I'd like to meet in a particular industry, I will contact a current or prior client in that same industry for intelligence and leverage that relationship in some way to meet this individual.

Do you do any commercial selling, or just leasing? If you sell, do you only sell the same type of property you lease, or do you evaluate what comes your way?

I assist with both the leasing and selling of office properties only. However, given the market in which I operate, leasing is far more common and accounts for a heavy majority of my activities and transactions.

What sort of things do you do to retain loyalty from your past clients?

I follow up with my clients on a quarterly basis, or take them to lunch, to see how their space or building is working out, and I return calls and emails quickly whenever they need assistance.

What do you do to keep up with current lease rates in your area?

Because of my level of transactions I am fortunate to have similar comps in a specific submarket by transactions I've done and been

190   *Chapter 17*

a part of, or else I can call one of my peers for information, or those who are a part of the CBRE office team to assist. Our brokerage office team represents a large percentage of the transactions in this community.

About how many hours a week do you work, on average?

My typical day is 7:30 a.m. to 5:30 p.m. with a half day off on Friday. This varies, but 40 to 50 hours a week is a fairly good estimate. It was much more than this earlier in my career because at that time I knew a lot about nothing!

Bruce, if I were a new licensee, and I just met you and asked you for advice on how to become a success in commercial real estate, what advice would you give me?

I would tell you to pick a specialty, work hard, be yourself, have fun, bring a great attitude to work each and every day, treat people fairly and professionally, and return every phone call. You never know who is on the other line!

Thank you, Bruce. I really appreciate you sharing your time and knowledge with us!

Pete Peterson

CEO and Partner
Stratton Group Real Estate of Keller Williams Southern Arizona
(520) 405-0086
petebpeterson@gmail.com

Pete, please tell our readers what brought you into real estate, and how and when you started.

In 2004 I decided to get my Arizona real estate license. I moved to Arizona in 1998, and had purchased three mobile home parks. I had previously worked as a regional sales manager for two different companies in the manufactured housing industry. I realized while working for these companies that I would make a very good living there but would not be able to build the wealth and freedom I desired. I saw there would not be a ceiling for creating wealth in a real estate career.

My job required me to interface with retain street dealers and in-park dealers. I did some investigating and saw the great return on investment with low fixed overhead expenses with this asset type. So in 1998 I resigned from my Pennsylvania job and went in as a partner on three turnaround mobile home park projects here in Tucson and moved my family here to begin our new journey.

The agent we used to buy these properties was a nice guy but didn't provide great representation, market knowledge, or skill, and certainly not in mobile homes, so we turned the properties around and I went into real estate in your office, with the mindset to specialize in mobile home parks. At first my focus was on commercial real estate, which gave me the opportunity to give great service while giving me the opportunity to acquire more income-producing properties.

Understanding that I needed time to work *on* my business as well as *in* my business, I became very aware that I only wanted to work with a partner, so I brought Angie Kuzma on board as a partner. She became our chief operating officer. Her role is *implementer* while mine is *vision, expansion, and growth.* We make a fantastic team. Her strengths compensated for my weaknesses. Her amazing and very different perspective has allowed us to debate strategic business decisions from different viewpoints. We launched the Stratton Group, and within two years moved our closed sales volume to $69 million. Our first year we focused

192   *Chapter 17*

on lead generation, year 2 we focused on building systems, and now, in our third year, we are focusing on growing our agents' production and expansion into new markets. We currently have 13 commercial brokers, and each has been required to choose a specialization in either mobile home parks, multifamily, or retail investments.

Pete, tell us what got you interested in specializing heavily in mobile home parks.

While I was searching for investment properties that met my needs, I realized that there were very few brokers who understood the product and that there were not a lot of options for great representation in that specialty. Shortly after I activated my license, I realized that it would be easy to get lost as a generalist in commercial real estate, and if I would specialize, investors would gladly pay me for my knowledge and experience. My journey took me into multifamily brokerage, and then into leadership roles in the industry, before opening the Stratton Group.

When and why did you decide to create a team?

After joining Keller Williams Commercial and becoming CEO of Keller Williams Southern Arizona, my primary duty was to grow the company as well as develop top-level talent and high-producing agents in the offices. Business development and coaching! I began to look at real estate from a different perspective. I was coaching agents to *build businesses, not just sell real estate.* Selling real estate is your job until you can replace yourself with a team member who can do that job better than you can. After three years I went back into production as a business owner, not as a salesperson, which changed absolutely everything. I began focusing on creating replicable systems that would allow me to upscale in volume, customer service, and attraction of talented people into our business.

Conversations with Three Veteran Commercial Brokers 193

For the first seven years of my career I really didn't understand the gift of leverage and how I could use it. My primary focus was being a great salesperson and real estate broker, and not looking as a business owner. I finally began to clearly understand the powerful concept of having a written business plan for working in my business as well as on my business. I suddenly realized that I really didn't have a business if I had to rely on me for production; I only had a job. I knew I had a business when I could leave for extended periods of time and we still had closings, new clients added to our database, and new agents joining our team.

Angie and I made a decision to create a team of specialists, each with a specific job they need to master: a financial analyst to handle offering memorandums; a marketing coordinator for any marketing and related collateral material; a transaction coordinator to help draft, move, and facilitate communication and documents to all parties to a transaction; inside sales associates that are on the phone doing lead generation for our senior associates (OSAs) and expansion partners in other cities. Leverage!

How many teams do you have, and in what states?

The model we run for the commercial side of our business is a one-team model with a hub in Tucson. From there we add expansion partners or expansion teams, and a selling agent or agents in other cities. Each expansion partner must specialize in one product type so we can help him/her build a database. Our goal is to create expansion pods physically set in Keller Williams offices around the country with each pod consisting of two multifamily specialists, two retail specialists, and one or two seasoned brokers to handle commercial referrals from the residential brokers in each office we expand into. Our 2018 goal is to have expansion partners in 18 locations with each location having at least one specialist in each of the three areas mentioned. We have currently expanded into California, Arizona, Texas, and Oklahoma.

Pete, will you please elaborate on what you feel are the advantages and disadvantages of being on a team?

People who understand the value and benefit of being in a team environment and thrive in that type of environment are our best candidates. Lone wolves won't find our culture a great fit. Angie and I believe the most important thing we have to offer is our culture. The environment and opportunities we create for growth and leadership for our agents is the driving force of our organization. There is such power in surrounding yourself with highly motivated, growth-minded, opportunity-based people who have a desire to build big businesses and give back to their community. It's a real driver for us!

Do you prefer new agents or experienced agents, and why?

There is a gift in having a mix of seasoned agents and new agents on our teams. With our coaching, training, and requirement for specialization, we really create a winning environment for new as well as seasoned agents to thrive, and enjoy the process. We have been very intentional about bringing on interns from our local colleges and the University of Arizona, with the idea of creating a pipeline of young, new talent onto our teams. Seasoned agents sometimes need to unwind some bad habits they have developed, but our requirement for specialization and our focus on prospecting and database building seem to work very well.

How do you feel about hiring experienced residential agents as team members, and, if you do, how long does it take them to commit to the switch?

The gift that residential agents bring to our team is that they are used to a faster-paced transaction. They tend to move with a sense of urgency in the escrow process as they are used to much shorter timelines. They understand the real estate escrow process, and

Conversations with Three Veteran Commercial Brokers 195

that gives them an edge over new agents. They only need to learn the product and have great coaching and mentoring to be quite successful. We have found that having coaching and mentoring available for these agents works very well. The main issue we have with them is that they sometimes want to continue their residential real estate activities while trying to launch a successful commercial real estate career, and that is very difficult to do! We set a definite timeline to close their residential business and become fully immersed in commercial real estate, and that seems to work best. If they won't commit to doing that, we don't hire them.

If I were a somewhat experienced residential agent with a very decent sales track record and I came to interview with you about joining your team, what sort of questions would you ask?

We have a system we use for our hiring process called "recruit/select" or "career visioning." This process comes with a whole series of questions that are created, based on the candidate taking a comprehensive personality profile test that allows us to focus on questions that will help us get to know that person at a deeper level. We also go into a deep discussion of their life, looking for trends of success and times of hardship and how they handled them. Our goal is to really get to know the person, understand their path in life, and look for patterns we feel will make them a good fit for our organization.

You have teams in four or five different states. How do you and Angie maintain control of the entire operation?

The biggest challenge with having expansion teams or partners is making sure they feel valued and connected to our hub in Tucson. We have online weekly sales meetings that everyone can access as well as Friday Fail Forward conference calls where we talk about our failures, and we also share everyone's "big win" for the week. We use the GroupMe app for daily nonverbal communication

196   *Chapter 17*

about daily motivational quotes, meeting reminders, and celebrating new appointments, new contracts, and new closings. We focus on lead indicators from a production standpoint rather than lag indicators, to make sure our expansion partners are tracking toward their goals.

You have an in-house lead generator referred to as an ISA, or inside sales administrator. How do you disburse the leads that person generates?

We run the inside sales model of our team. We have inside sales administrators, better known as ISAs, that have specific geographical areas that they are assigned to call on specific days of the week. Their job is to nurture potential sellers until they are ready to release financials and rent rolls. Then we introduce them to the expansion partner for that area, and the handoff is made between inside and outside sales.

What type of accountability issues are the team members responsible for, and how do you enforce them?

We use the 411 for goal planning, and the agents are required to update it every week. [411 is a business planning tool that requires the users to write down the four most pressing issues they are currently dealing with, select the most pressing issue, and write the primary action necessary to resolve it.] Using this in conjunction with peer accountability has been a very effective tool for keeping the agents focused on the most important thing in their business: finding new business opportunities. We also do a one-on-one productivity coaching for brand new agents, with mentor oversight on their initial transactions. Angie and I have strived hard to weave accountability into every aspect of our business so the agents take 100% ownership of their business and the outcomes. End-of-day staff reports on key matrix issues such as contacts added to our

Conversations with Three Veteran Commercial Brokers   197

database, contracts written, contracts accepted, and escrows opened and closed let us see who is working effectively and who needs additional coaching or the supervision and help of a mentor.

If I were a new agent just starting with you, what direction and training would you direct me to, and why?

We are currently in the process of creating a written program for new agents that includes recorded video content on best practices, skill training, and system operations that is delivered automatically with a client retention module that we had built for our teams. Really exploring what specialty really interests the new agent is also quite important, and getting them into a relationship with a mentor and coach is imperative. They are going to pay for training, either by losing transactions and opportunities they would have gotten with experienced help or [by] investing in [education of their craft] through coaching and development.

There is an old saying that "if you don't have an assistant, you are one." Being part of a dynamic team solves this because you get to leverage away nonproductive or low-production issues to someone else who likes that kind of task, and focus on the tasks that you enjoy and make you money.

I am always open to and have learned that masterminding with my peers that are implementing new and innovative systems and models is an excellent source of continued learning for everyone in our organization, including Angie and me.

Thank you, Pete. I really appreciate your time and your insights into what makes a team successful!

198   *Chapter 17*

Paul Lindsey, CCIM

Retired President of Coldwell Banker Success Southwest
Tucson, Arizona
Paul@plindsey.com

Paul, please tell the readers a little about your background.

I began my real estate career in 1982 with a small full-service company. In those days, full service meant everyone got to do everything because there was no such thing as specialization. I got my broker license in three years, and formed a commercial investment company with several local businessmen as clients, and struck out on my own.

After two years I began to feel isolated from the people and information that are so important to the business, and I joined a growing commercial company as their number 2 leader. We grew the company to become the largest in our market, but by 1989 I began to feel restless again.

Three of us from that company plus two other well-respected commercial brokers formed Chapman/Lindsey Commercial Brokerage. I was the designated broker. We each specialized in certain product areas, with me as the main commercial investment broker. One of the other brokers focused on commercial property asset management, two others on land, and [another] on retail leasing and brokerage.

In 1999, I was given the opportunity to bring Chapman/Lindsey into a partnership with the local Coldwell Banker franchise as its commercial division. My partners balked at the move, but I saw it as a tremendous opportunity and left in the fall to become a 50% owner of the Coldwell Banker company, which was 99% residential, and still is. We grew the company from about $9 million in gross

Conversations with Three Vetera.

commissions to about $40 million, greatly assis
est real estate market in history. In March 2005
alty Trust (NRT), which is Cendant's real estate ho.
made us a generous offer, and the decision to sell wa.

When you entered real estate, what made you decide to become a commercial broker instead of a residential broker?

My first broker encouraged me to do whatever interested me and supported me in exploring commercial brokerage and leasing. My prior life had been mostly business related, and most of my sphere of influence was the business community. I sold a few houses, but it became clear early on that the challenge and complexity of the commercial brokerage world was where my passion rested. I was also lucky enough to have a wife with a steady salary!

Paul, what type of training did you receive?

I would take any commercial classes the local schools would offer, but there weren't many, and the quality was spotty. I started the CCIM classes right away, although I had to wait several years to build the portfolio of transactions needed to earn the designation. I found the classes extremely interesting, and the people who attended were of a consistently high quality. By 1988 I had earned the CCIM designation. At that time there were only about 3,000 in the entire industry, and only eight in Tucson.

> You know, I took CI 101 through 104 in 1987 and had the portfolio to get the designation, but I was running my own company then, and I didn't want to go to NAR (National Association of REALTORS®) headquarters in Chicago to take the last course. I have so often wished I would have completed the last course and achieved the CCIM designation!

aul, what are your thoughts on specialization in one type of commercial real estate instead of trying to do it all, like we used to do?

I always suggest that agents make every effort to specialize, but sometimes that means trying several things before you find the one that feels right for you. Possessing more information than the competition gives you an enormous advantage that only comes with specialization.

When you started, what type of preparation did you do? Did you build a comp book, drive the territory to learn where the various commercial properties were located, determine which properties had which type of tenants, and so on?

Our market has always had a very cooperative fraternity, with agents very willing to share information. Like most cities, we never had a commercial MLS [multiple listing service], so access to the commercial listings was always a challenge. Building strong relationships within the brokerage community is the best single step an agent can take. Keeping records of the entire inventory of your geographic area and specialty in some organized way is critical, especially for leasing agents. Being able to access information about the size, ownership, tenant mix, and so on, of your market properties is basic, but critical to success!

In what way were you trained to acquire new clients and retain the loyalty of your current and past clients?

I was always told that integrity should always be your strongest suit, and I believe that passionately to this day! You also need for your client to know, without a doubt, that you are his or her strongest advocate in the adventure, and always have his or her best interest at heart. Nothing can replace repeat business!

Conversations with Three Veteran Commercial Brokers 201

Paul, what is your advice about creating and sticking to an annual business plan?

A business plan is primarily important because it helps you organize your time. In our market there are only so many commercial opportunities that an agent can handle at any given time, unlike a residential agent who can handle a dozen escrows at once, with help, so time management is very important. Making your calls, updating your files, keeping current with your literature, and staying abreast of the changes in the marketplace from local to national are a must.

What are some key points in the successful preparation for a listing presentation with a prospective seller?

Being totally prepared for a commercial listing presentation involves knowing more than the client, and more than the competition in terms of other properties on the market, trends in that specialty area, pending re-zoning or developments, recent sales or leases, and suggestions for improving the property for a quicker and higher sale. The client has to be convinced that you will be his advocate throughout the entire process.

What are the critical steps and issues to be thinking about or to cover as you conduct the interview with the sellers?

The first things on the sellers' minds are:

1. What is my property worth?

2. How marketable is my property?

3. What do I need to do to enhance its value and marketability?

202   *Chapter 17*

In the back of their mind is always whether they will make a profit on the sale and how much, but that is often a question they will not openly share with you. The broker's honesty and candor are always the key to his credibility; therefore, telling the seller what the market is saying, and not necessarily what they want to hear, is sometimes difficult, but always critically important. Setting out a marketing plan with accountability built in and timelines for execution of your activities is also very important.

Writing a commercial purchase contract can be very different than writing a standard residential contract. What are some of the key issues that you feel are important to have fully covered in the commercial contract?

The commercial contract is always more complicated than the residential contract as it will often include tenant issues, ownership issues, legal issues, a lengthy feasibility study or due diligence period with many steps, more complicated lending issues, and a longer escrow closing period, and purchase contracts drafted by buyers' attorneys. The preprinted contracts that most real estate associations provide are excellent templates to work from. Some states require an attorney to be involved instead of an escrow agent. The seller and buyer may each have tax issues that need to be addressed and will often require the review and approval of their respective tax and/or legal advisor. The settlement statements will usually involve proration of leasehold income, various assessments, prepaid fees, and various other items that can make the statements much more complicated, and the preliminary title report can involve many exclusions that may need to be addressed.

How much should a commercial agent know about Internal Revenue Code Section 1031 tax-deferred exchanges?

A good commercial agent should be very familiar with the 1031 tax-deferred exchange provisions of the tax code. Giving your

Conversations with Three Veteran Commercial Brokers **203**

client a good overview of their options is quite important as there can be dire tax consequences for your client if they are not properly informed. You need to be aware that many accountants have little or no practical knowledge of these provisions, and your client should always ask the accountant if they are familiar with that code section. The agent must be very careful to not give tax advice, but give the client enough knowledge to be able to seek advice from a competent tax advisor.

Do you feel it is wise to have the clients' attorney or tax counsel either draft the purchase agreement or, if you draft it, make it contingent on their approval?

In most cases your client will probably be looking to you to draft the purchase agreement for them, especially in those states where preprinted forms are available. You are always wise to suggest that your client have their attorney review the contract, and to suggest they involve their tax counsel in any calculations or to help structure the transaction so it works to the client's advantage from a tax standpoint.

Please tell us your feelings about the value of proper training, mentoring, and guidance.

Clients can sense insecurity, and if you are not confident, well informed, and fully prepared for a meeting with them, then you will probably not do as well as you would have liked. That sense of confidence that all clients desire in their broker comes from a combination of training and preparation. Unfortunately, most communities do not have adequate training for commercial brokers, so unless you are with a firm that has developed its own training and mentoring system, you are pretty much on your own. If that applies to any of the folks reading this, I suggest they contact the National Association of REALTORS® and get started with the CCIM courses.

204 *Chapter 17*

It is really hard to beat the experience you can quickly gain by shadowing a seasoned broker or working with a mentor in your office. If there is no training for commercial agents in the office you are with, it may be time to find one that has it available. Always talk to your broker first, tell him or her of your needs, and see what he or she is willing to do about it before you make a move. *By far, the agents who make the most money year after year are the ones that get with one company and office and build their entire career there, so choose carefully!*

What are the typical success patterns you look for in a newly developing commercial agent?

They are unmistakable. The ones who are on the road to success get it! They plan their time carefully. They willingly prospect for new business and to build their client base. They ask a lot of questions. They are open to bringing in an experienced agent to assist on a transaction they aren't totally comfortable with, and they seek knowledge constantly.

What do you see as the most important thing an agent or firm can do to remain successful?

It's really this simple: control the inventory. There is an old saying in real estate that goes right to the heart of a successful career: "Those that list last!" There is also a secondary thing that works well but may leave an agent vulnerable to the whims of the marketplace: control the buyers, and in this day and age it is perfectly reasonable on the agent's part to require the buyer to sign a Buyer/Broker Agreement where the buyer signs a listing agreement that says the broker gets paid no matter who the buyer buys through for the duration of the listing.

Paul, what are the three best tips or pieces of advice you can give to the reader of this book to help him/her make a decision to enter the commercial real estate field successfully?

1. Do you have the temperament to deal with failure and rejection on a fairly regular basis and keep optimistic and positive? The percentage of commercial transactions that actually close is considerably less than in residential sales, so time will be spent unsuccessfully more often.

2. Do you have the financial resources to sustain yourself and perhaps your family for many months until commission checks start to come your way? The single most intense pressure is that which comes from the financial stress of not having a predictable income stream. It is much more difficult to create an income rhythm in commercial real estate because the escrows are usually so much longer and the times at bat are fewer, although the proliferation of teams where an agent is fed leads by a prospecting specialist seem to mitigate that a lot.

3. Do you enjoy being with people? The most successful real estate people are those that are working all the time. By that I mean their work is so integrated into the rest of their lives that there is no clear division between working and not working. If you can get to the point where you are enjoying being with your clients and customers regardless of the time of day, your success will be assured.

Paul, I want to really thank you for your words of wisdom. You have given some wonderful insight into the life of a commercial broker, and it is appreciated!

206   *Chapter 17*

Review Questions

1. Which of the following issues do Bruce Suppes and Paul Lindsey totally agree on?
   A. seeking out the perfect firm and office for you and staying there your entire career
   B. transferring from office to office because you will get referrals from more agents that way
   C. moving to a different branch within your own company once or twice to rejuvenate your interest in the business
   D. staying with an office that doesn't support you properly but telling the broker what needs to be changed

2. At CBRE, Bruce Suppes had which of the following options?
   A. He was allowed to choose the product type he wished to pursue.
   B. The branch manager directed him to retail shopping center brokerage.
   C. The designated broker directed him to office leasing and sales.
   D. He chose not to specialize.

3. Which of the following statements about Bruce Suppes is true?
   A. He always works alone.
   B. He always works with a partner.
   C. When the situation warrants, he works with two brokers in his office as partners.
   D. none of the answer choices

4. Which of the following statements about Pete Peterson is NOT true?
   A. He believes in the use of a mentor and a coach for his agents.
   B. He is expanding into many different states.
   C. He believes in the "narrow and deep" philosophy.
   D. Currently he does not have any expansion partners.

5. Which commercial real estate product does Pete Peterson personally specialize in?
   A. mobile home parks
   B. the sale of mobile homes
   C. multifamily properties
   D. self-storage properties that allow mobile home parking

Class Discussion Topics

1. Consider and talk about the advantages and disadvantages of staying with one firm your entire career versus moving from firm to firm.
2. What are the advantages and disadvantages of specializing in commercial leasing over commercial sales?
3. Discuss the advantages and disadvantages of working on a commercial real estate team as compared with working solo.
4. Name the support positions that Pete Peterson has in his Tucson hub, and describe the purpose and value of each one.
5. According to Paul Lindsey, what is the most important thing a firm can do to remain viable in any marketplace, and what sort of activities accomplish it?

Part 2

Commercial Real Estate Investment Types

18. **Single-Family Homes and Condominiums:
    A Great Place to Start**

19. **Multifamily Complexes, Large and Small**

20. **Office Buildings**

21. **Retail Shopping Centers**

22. **Self-Storage Facilities**

23. **Single-Tenant NNN-Leased Investments**

24. **Land Brokerage**

25. **Mobile Home Parks**

26. **Industrial Properties**

Chapter 18

Single-Family Homes and Condominiums: A Great Place to Start

212   *Chapter 18*

Many individuals enter the investment real estate market by acquiring single-family homes or condominiums. There are both advantages and disadvantages to starting with this type of investment, and much of it has to do with the investor's temperament and investment goals.

Advantages

- *high leverage.* Today's real estate market has a multitude of lenders that will readily make 80% and even 90% loans on rental homes or condominiums. Few homes or condominiums (condos) will have a cash flow at 90% loan-to-value ratio (LTV), so if the buyer wants to leverage that much, he/she will need to have a very high FICO score, a strong financial statement, and ample cash reserves available. With low-to-moderate interest rates, most lower- and mid-priced homes and condos will break even at 75 to 80% LTVs. When investing in condos and single-family homes in planned unit developments (PUDs), be careful to include the monthly homeowners association dues in your cash-flow analysis, given that some monthly homeowners association assessments are prohibitively high.

  If you are going to obtain financing in excess of 80%, look into getting an 80% first loan and a lender 15-year second loan for the balance of the required financing. This will avoid your having to pay for private mortgage insurance, which is not tax deductible, and the rapid payoff of the second loan helps to build equity faster. See your accountant about this.

- *rapid appreciation.* Single-family homes and many condos tend to appreciate faster than other types of real estate investments, especially if you own one during one of the periods of ultra-rapid housing inflation seen in the past several years.

  Many investors have seen their equity double or triple in a year during these times. An investor who plans to acquire a

Single-Family Homes and Condominiums: A Great Place to Start   **213**

home per year for three years in an area that has a history of high appreciation may, within five or six years, very well find himself/herself in a position to trade up to a small apartment house that will support professional management. A word of caution here: In recent years the market has fluctuated wildly, and overleveraging a property or purchasing too many too fast may result in a significant loss if the market turns on the investor. Do not purchase beyond your very safe cash reserves!

- *large resale market.* The demand for resale homes and condos creates the largest real estate market in the United States. When it is time to dispose of the home as an investment, there is usually a large buyer pool ready to buy it if it is in good condition and priced appropriately. Be sure to offer the property to the tenant first when selling, because many tenants are avidly ready to buy and prefer not to move—but get them pre-approved for financing before you enter into a purchase/sale contract with them.

- *ease of management.* Single-family homes and condos are usually easy to manage. The largest group of prospective tenants is usually families, and through careful screening you can usually get a tenant who will take reasonably good care of the property. Because there is usually only one tenant, there is only one rent to collect and very few monthly bills to pay, so bookkeeping is easy. If you invest in a property near a college, then you may very well have multiple tenants and get higher-than-normal rents, but students are notorious for being hard on rentals.

Disadvantages

- *lack of cash flow.* Single-family homes and condos seldom produce enough rent to provide a meaningful cash flow unless the buyer pays 30% or more as down payment. The reduced

214 *Chapter 18*

leverage tends to lower the cash-on-cash return on the investment.

- *potentially higher vacancy rate.* Since there is usually only one tenant, the property is not bringing in any income if the tenant is not paying the rent or while it is vacant. There is no way to effectively spread the financial risk through multiple tenants. If you do rent to more than one tenant, be sure each person is named on the lease because this makes each person individually as well as collectively liable for rent payments.

- *rent control.* Many cities and counties have rent control ordinances that must be identified *before* acquiring any residential income property, including rental homes and condos. Rent control can sharply limit the owner's ability to maintain a cash flow that is equal to or ahead of inflation.

- *potential management issues.* Many excellent professional management firms are available that will take over complete rental and management duties of single-family homes and condos, usually for about 8 to 10% of collected rents. If you can't afford one of these firms, then you will be required to pay landlord. This can be anything from a pleasant to a frightful experience. In 1973, I hired a young Filipino guy who had just started specializing in investment sales. He decided to manage the properties he sold. He came in one afternoon, and although he had a dark complexion, he was as white as a sheet and told me that a tenant had put a gun to his head when he knocked on the door and asked for the rent. He quickly decided to turn the property management duties over to other professionals.

He came in one afternoon as white as a sheet and told me that a tenant had put a gun to his head.

Single-Family Homes and Condominiums: A Great Place to Start   215

You can sometimes end up with long-term tenants. This is good and bad. You avoid vacancies that way, but long-term tenants often expect rent concessions in return, which can affect your cash flow. This won't affect the property's value as it would another type of income-producing property because the new buyer is usually not buying the property for its ability to produce income; the buyer wants a home to live in. A good way to handle a long-term tenant is to inform him/her you intend to raise the rent every year, but you will keep the rent a little below the going market rate for as long as the tenant stays. If tenants are told this right up front, they usually go along with it.

- *maintenance.* Most condos are easy to maintain because you only have to worry about the interior of the unit. The offset of this, of course, is the association dues you pay, which include reserves for roof replacement and other periodic structural maintenance that may not occur during your ownership. Single-family homes are a little different; they usually include lawns, shrubbery, and fences to maintain, as well as exterior and interior paint. Many tenants do not do a stellar job of maintaining homes the way an owner would. You need to be accepting of this, or it will drive you crazy. Think twice about buying a rental home with a swimming pool—it's probably not a good idea. If you do invest in one, always rent it with pool service included with no exceptions, even if the prospective tenant tells you he/she does his/her own pool maintenance now. Renting a home with a gardener included is fairly easy to do; I've done so with some of the rentals I've owned over the years, and it has worked out fine. Accept the fact that when you sell the property, you will probably have to spend some money getting the property in shape.

Think twice about buying a rental home with a swimming pool.

216 Chapter 18

- *tenant issues when selling.* As stated earlier, you will usually end up with a family or a single person as your tenant with this type of investment. They are never happy about receiving news from you that you are selling the property. It is not uncommon for the tenant to become uncooperative and make showing the property extremely difficult, if not impossible.

You have three choices:

1. You can wait out the tenant's lease and give the tenant the required 30-days' notice to vacate, get the tenant out, refurbish the property, and then market it vacant. Some properties show better when they are vacant; some show worse. If you have a sloppy tenant or a very uncooperative one, this is always the best course of action if at all possible.

2. You can adhere to the terms of the lease and the landlord-tenant laws of your state and give the tenant the required notice prior to each showing of the property. (This is cumbersome, however, and difficult to do with an uncooperative tenant and can sometimes lead to open confrontation.)

3. You can negotiate with the tenant and thereby create a win-win situation. See the tenant personally to state your need to sell the property, and then offer a small concession of $75 to $200 a month off the rent. Tell the tenant that all showings will be by appointment only with a minimum two hours' notice unless the tenant is not home; then you will personally meet all agents and buyers wanting to see the property in the tenant's absence. Assure the tenant you will provide a minimum of 45 days' notice before the tenant must vacate. (If you do this, be sure to construct the offer you receive to reflect the proper timing for the tenant's notice.) Do *not* put a keybox (also referred to as a "lockbox") on the property because doing so may violate the Landlord-

Single-Family Homes and Condominiums: A Great Place to Start 217

Tenant Act regulations requiring the landlord to give the required notice prior to showing the property, even if the tenant agrees to it. The notice period varies from state to state. California's is 48 hours, for example. Check your state and local ordinances.

Review Questions

1. Which of the following is usually the easiest to self-manage?
   A. 10-unit apartment complex
   B. triplex
   C. NNN-leased seven-unit strip center
   D. condominium

2. A group of four out-of-state college students wants to rent your single-family home. How are you as the owner best protected legally?
   A. require the parents with the best financial statement to cosign for the students
   B. have the student with the highest FICO score sign the lease
   C. require each student to be of legal age and to sign the lease as jointly and severally liable
   D. just give the students a month-to-month rental agreement

3. What is the biggest disadvantage of owning a single-family home as a rental?
   A. When the tenant leaves, there is no income.
   B. Tenants often are not great about doing yard work.
   C. Single-family-home tenants complain more frequently and about smaller things.
   D. The tenants may make showing the property to others difficult.

218   *Chapter 18*

4. What is the best way to sell a condo when you have a trouble-
    some tenant who doesn't want to move?
    A. start eviction proceedings immediately
    B. wait out the lease and give the tenant the required 30-days'
            written notice to vacate
    C. call the local sheriff's office and file a complaint
    D. threaten to throw him/her out

5. What is the best way to get a tenant's cooperation in showing
    the property when you want to sell it but the tenant still has
    four months left on the lease?
    A. notify the tenant in writing that you are breaking the lease
    B. offer a slightly reduced rent and at least a 45-days' notice
            that you have sold the property
    C. offer to pay a small sum toward the tenant's moving ex-
            penses
    D. both B and C answer choices

Class Discussion Topics

1. You have saved enough for the down payment and closing
    costs on a small investment, but you are just not into rehabili-
    tative landscaping. What is probably the best real estate invest-
    ment for you, and why?
2. The rental market is strong for apartments and single-family
    homes. Your main goal is to increase your net worth. What is
    probably your best investment, and why?
3. What are the advantages of self-managing a single-family-
    home investment?
4. What are the disadvantages of condo ownership as a rental?
5. What steps are involved in evicting a tenant, and in what order
    should they be taken?

Chapter 19

Multifamily Complexes, Large and Small

220   *Chapter 19*

When talking about apartment complexes in this chapter, I include everything from a duplex up to a large apartment complex with several hundred units. They all have a common theme: They provide shelter for people to live in and provide an income for the nonresident owner. In certain areas, they are also subject to rent control ordinances, so check your area's regulations carefully.

Smaller units such as duplexes, triplexes, and four-unit buildings are sometimes owner occupied and can provide the owner with a place to live and an income at the same time. The drawback to such an arrangement is that the tenants often feel that because the owner lives right there, it is all right to contact the owner at all hours and about the smallest issues. The owner's personality usually dictates how long to endure that kind of intrusion before moving elsewhere or laying down the law to the tenants. This type of arrangement can be an excellent retirement-planning vehicle for many people, and financing for two- to four-unit buildings is somewhat cheaper and easier than financing properties with five or more units. In the real estate investment world, two- to four-unit properties are classified as residential income properties, and five or more units are classified as multifamily income properties.

Buildings containing five or more units are rarely owner occupied and are normally held for tax shelter and/or production of income. They can normally be financed to a maximum of 75% of their value, but someone with a very strong financial statement can often get an 80% loan. They are not readily financed by lenders that finance owner-occupied one- to four-unit buildings. Builders sometimes build smaller units like this (from five to 15 units) in pairs with a common driveway between them. If you, as an agent, ever list such a building, one of your first marketing activities should be to contact the owner of the building across the driveway to see if he/she would like to expand his/her holdings. Most often, these types of buildings have a recorded "mutual maintenance agreement" that calls for both owners to share maintenance and repairs of the driveway. It can be a source of irritation to an owner who maintains his/her property to share a driveway with an owner who doesn't; and if the unmaintained building is placed for sale, the owner across the driveway is often a motivated buyer. Most buildings of this size are non-amenity, with no swimming pool, recreation room, or exercise room, but there are a few exceptions.

Many states, including California, require a resident manager for buildings that contain 16 units or more.

Buildings with about 20 or more units will very often have amenities such as swimming pools, recreation rooms, technology (Wi-Fi) rooms, fitness centers, and larger, comfortable lobbies where tenants can spend time. As these buildings start to become three-story, elevators become commonplace. Elevators entail a rather expensive additional operating cost, so be very careful to look into annual maintenance fees and repairs when you are performing an analysis of a building with an elevator or swimming pool. In many areas, it is common to see an apartment complex of several hundred units that is composed of many 20- to 50-unit buildings. As a result of the rising cost of homes, these types of buildings and complexes have been the favorite target of condominium (condo) conversion specialists.

> Be very careful to look into annual maintenance fees and repairs when you are performing an analysis of a building with an elevator or swimming pool.

Single buildings of 60 to 150 units are considered midrise apartment complexes and can be several stories high. Buildings of this size usually have an attractive lobby and amenities such as pools, spas, and fitness centers. They are also large enough to support a

222 Chapter 19

part-time or full-time maintenance staff. This may comprise one person or several, depending on the age, size, and condition of the building. These buildings are almost always managed by a professional property management company and have a separate office for the resident manager.

Buildings over 150 units are sometimes in the high-rise category and may contain many stories. Like the midrise buildings, they have a full-time support and maintenance staff, employ a resident manager, and are professionally managed. They, too, have a high number of amenities. They are often located in urban downtown areas, and the first floor usually consists of retail shops and boutiques, while the second through third or fourth floors are often office space, with the remainder being residential apartments—and, of course, they all have elevators.

There is usually an inverse relationship between the location of an apartment complex and its capitalization (cap) rate: The better the location, the lower the cap rate. This means that an apartment complex in an old, declining area of town would usually sell at a higher cap rate than the same apartment complex would in a nicer area of town. It has to do with the risk/reward factor. Remember, a higher cap rate means a higher financial return to the owner and a lower value, given the same net operating income, because you divide the net operating income by the cap rate to arrive at the property's value.

Apartment house brokerage is the area of commercial real estate where most agents work. It is the best understood area because of its similarities to residential home brokerage, and more agents are familiar with the landlord-tenant issues involved in apartment house sales than they are with other commercial real estate sales.

If you decide to specialize in apartment house brokerage of any size (and, yes, there is a very good living to be made in the smaller ones!), have your local title company get you a list of all the ownership records in your area for the type or size units you are going to specialize in. There may be a small charge for this because of the Real Estate Settlement Procedures Act (RESPA) Section 8 restrictions. The list will have the site address, which is the address of the building you hope to market one day; it will also have the mailing address, which is the owner's mailing address. If the property is owned by a limited liability company (LLC), corporation, or other holding entity, you will have to search your state's secretary of state website or the county records to get the name of an actual contact person. Add these contacts to your database and start mailing and calling. Your first mailing should be an introductory letter from you that includes your résumé, if appropriate, and a statement informing them that you are expanding your client base by X number of multifamily property owners and would like to include them in all your future mailings. Include a printout from either CoStar or LoopNet of recent sales and/or current listings that closely match what they already own. Also, with every mailing be sure to include your business card with all your contact information. Be consistent; mail every month in the beginning and allow it plenty of time; the contacts need to get to know you before they will deal with you, and this can take several months, but the process is time tested and works every time. This process applies to every commercial real estate product. One way that most often leads to a listing sooner rather than later is to drive the area where your target properties are located and look for properties that are run-down or in a state of noticeable disrepair. Take a digital picture of the property, print it out, and mail it to the owners. Let them know that you work the area their property is in, you saw the condition of their property, and you wanted to let them know about it. Offer to help them rehabilitate the property, sell it, or exchange it for another. The picture often results in an email or phone call from out-of-state owners saying they had no idea the property management company they are using had let the property get so bad; they may ask you to help them rehabilitate the

224   *Chapter 19*

property and then sell it. Use your title company as a resource; its staff are there to help. Just be sure that you reward their efforts with some business.

> Use your title company as a resource; its staff are there to help.

Review Questions

1. The main drawback to living in a unit of residential income property you own is that:
   A. you are automatically not eligible for any tax shelter
   B. the tenants are lax about paying the rent on time
   C. you can't get owner-occupied financing even if it is four units or less
   D. tenants feel that they can contact the owners at any time, night or day, about any little thing

2. Which of the following statements is true?
   A. An investor with a small bank account and a 650 FICO score would probably be able to get an 80% loan on a 60-unit multifamily property.
   B. An investor with an 830 FICO score, a six-figure bank account, and a high-paying job would probably be able to get an 80% loan on an 80-unit multifamily property.
   C. An investor with a 705 FICO score applying for a 25% loan with 75% down will probably not get the loan.
   D. none of the answer choices

Multifamily Complexes, Large and Small   225

3. Which of the following statements is true?
   A. Properties in somewhat desirable areas sell for more than similar properties in highly desirable areas.
   B. Properties in highly desirable areas sell for less than similar properties in undesirable areas.
   C. Properties in highly desirable areas sell for the same value as similar properties in somewhat desirable and undesirable areas.
   D. Properties in undesirable areas are usually purchased at a higher cap rate than similar properties in highly desirable areas.

4. What is the benefit of asking the owners you are mailing to for their email address?
   A. Email is faster than "snail mail."
   B. Most investors look online for things that may affect their real estate, and they will almost surely look forward to your emails.
   C. Email is easier and less expensive than regular mail for conveying information to them continuously.
   D. all of the answer choices

5. Which of the following should be included in your first mailing to your new database?
   A. a personal letter introducing yourself, stating that you specialize in the type of property they own at (address), and letting them know you are expanding your client list by X number of people, and you would like to include them in all your future mailings about their type of property
   B. your business card and your résumé, if appropriate; information about your company if your résumé is weak at the time
   C. a short list of current listings and new sales in the metro area of the type of property they own
   D. all of the answer choices

226   *Chapter 19*

Class Discussion Topics

1. You got a call from Henry. He and his wife own a triplex in the central part of town. They are in their 80s, the property has no loan, and the area has declined significantly, with much drug trafficking; they aren't comfortable living there any longer. How would you advise them, and why?

2. A friend of yours calls you and tells you he wants to invest in a rental condominium that he will keep for two years and then exchange for a rental home in the same area. There have been a large number of condos on the market for several years, and the appreciation has been nil. How would you advise him?

3. Discuss the value of periodic mailings and emails to a specific client base. How often is this effective, what should the communications contain, and why would you include what you state is relevant?

4. You have decided to specialize in residential income property brokerage of two- to four-unit properties. What are the advantages of this specialty? What are the disadvantages?

5. You are creating a database of strip centers to specialize in. You plan on mailing to the owners on a monthly basis. What are the issues that you must consider before you proceed?

Chapter 20

Office Buildings

228   *Chapter 20*

Office buildings come in a wide variety of shapes and sizes, from a commercially zoned home that is converted to office use, to highrise buildings like the Empire State Building.

Depending on your client's needs, a commercially zoned home on a main thoroughfare may be just perfect, given that it can afford a great deal of privacy and high visibility. Insurance brokers, mortgage brokers, chiropractors, dentists, and other small-business owners tend to like the high visibility and easy access provided by this type of converted office space. There is usually ample room to accommodate the parking requirements of any city or county ordinances as well.

If you are representing a client in acquiring this type of space, you will need to be extremely careful about protecting their interests by looking into the current zoning as well as the need for any special-use permits that may be required. A home with commercial zoning is not automatically granted a use permit for any type of business, so carefully assess your client's needs and get him/her involved with the right people at the local planning and building departments. Be sure to include a contingency in any purchase offer you write for a client that says the sale is contingent on the property being approved for a use permit for the specific type of business your client wants to open.

A drawback of owning this type of property is expansion. If your client plans on expanding the business, you should caution him/her to assess the size of the building being considered to see if it fits into any mid- or long-term expansion plans. Adding on more space is expensive, and depending on setback ordinances and other limiting factors, the building under consideration may prove to be too small or the floor plan unworkable for the expansion your client has in mind.

Financing versus renting is also a consideration. When I owned my real estate company in the San Francisco Bay Area, for example,

Office Buildings **229**

I was strongly considering doing just what we have been talking about. In late 1979, I found a commercially zoned home in a very attractive location in town that was large enough to meet my business needs for several years to come. However, interest rates were climbing rapidly—they were approximately 12% at the time and, of course, went through the roof shortly thereafter. When I looked into financing, I found that my monthly after-tax ownership costs didn't make the move from my current location attractive at all.

Many small office buildings have 2,000 to 20,000 net-rentable square feet. A large number of these are privately owned, but many of the owners have formed a privately held limited liability company (LLC) or corporation and have deeded the building to that entity for various tax- and liability-limiting purposes. If you have access to your state's secretary of state website, you will easily be able to look up the name of a real person to communicate with; if not, you will need to do some digging through the county assessor's records to come up with a "person for service of notice, or managing partner." Every nonhuman form of property ownership, such as corporations, LLCs, Subchapter S corporations, and partnerships using a "doing business as" (DBA) form must file a form with the state's secretary of state that tells the public who is empowered by that entity to be served papers for legal proceedings or other types of written communication. That person or the managing partner will be your initial contact person.

These smaller office buildings have a wide variety of tenants that may include small real estate firms, mortgage brokerage firms, insurance brokers, and many other small businesses. The main advantage to the tenant of this type of office space instead of the converted home is the ability to expand without moving. My real estate company was in a neighborhood retail shopping center, and when the shoe store next door went out of business, I quickly took the space and expanded my operation.

230   *Chapter 20*

The location of these smaller office buildings varies widely, from marginal neighborhoods that are going through an economic downturn, to newly created neighborhoods that are thriving. The amount of rent charged will vary depending on vacancy rates, the strength of the economy, and the prosperity of the area where the building is located. While we are on the subject of rents, let's look at the various types of rent that can be charged for office space.

- *gross lease.* In a gross lease, the tenant pays only the actual rent for the square feet his/her business occupies. Each unit will usually be separately metered for utilities, but the owner pays all other operating costs of the property. On occasion, utilities are even included!

- *modified gross lease.* In a modified gross lease, the tenant pays the space rent, their own interior utilities, and janitorial; and the lease may or may not contain a provision whereby the tenant pays any increase in the taxes and insurance over the base year.

- *net-net-net lease.* Often referred to as an NNN lease or "triple-net" lease, these leases state that the tenant pays a proportional share of *all* operating costs of the property, including real estate taxes, insurance, building maintenance and repairs, and landscaping maintenance. Most are specific about CAM, or common-area maintenance, charges being paid by all tenants on a proportional basis that are usually tied to the percentage of square feet each tenant occupies compared with the total square footage of the building. With this type of lease, the owner passes through all operating expenses to the tenants. Some leases of this nature include a charge for professional property management, and others do not. It is best to be very specific about this issue.

Although some office space is leased on a month-to-month basis or a one-year lease, most office space is leased for several years at a

Office Buildings   231

time. To stay even with the rate of inflation, these leases have built-in rental increases that are usually tied to the annual percentage rise in the CPI for a given metropolitan area or are increased on an annual basis by a fixed percentage of the then-existing base rent, as stated earlier. You can find out what this figure is in your area by contacting your local chamber of commerce or checking with an experienced commercial agent. The CPI method has largely been phased out.

The age of the building will have an effect on the rents the owner can charge as well as on the operating expenses incurred by the owner, which may or may not be passed on to the tenants. Many, if not most, of these buildings have flat roofs coated with tar and gravel. It is important to build an annual fee into the operating budget of these buildings that allows for repairs each year and replacement every 12 or so years (this will vary in different parts of the country).

Office buildings of this type can be vulnerable to a downturn in the economy and to business failures. A downturn in the economy will sometimes cause a marginally successful business to start to lose revenue. If the business owner does not have sufficient cash reserves and the business stops producing enough income to pay all its operating expenses, including the rent, the owner may declare bankruptcy and go out of business, leaving the property owner with a nonpaying tenant or an extended vacancy. Owners of these types of office buildings are well advised to keep a reasonable cash reserve to cover loan payments and operating expenses in the event this happens. Generally, office buildings can be financed to only 65 to 70% of their value, and because they are commercial, they are depreciated over 39 years.

> Owners of these types of office buildings are well advised to keep a reasonable cash reserve.

232   *Chapter 20*

Many office buildings are in business parks. The entire park may be owned by one corporation, or each building may have an individual owner. If you are selling an office building in a business park, be careful to discover any association fees or other costs involved with ownership in the park as well as restrictions on signage. Most business parks have recorded covenants, conditions, and restrictions (CC&Rs). If you are involved in the purchase, sale, or lease of a property in a business park, ask your favorite title company to get you a copy of the CC&Rs. Read them, keeping in mind your client's needs, and look for anything that is detrimental to those needs. See that your client receives a copy of them in a format that proves you gave them to him/her (email the CC&Rs to the client and blind-copy yourself or make a copy and have the client sign for them along with the date).

As office buildings get larger, they tend to have lobbies and more amenities, much like those in apartment buildings. Many have conference rooms that can be reserved for use by the various businesses leasing space in them, and some have spas, fitness centers, boutiques, restaurants, and retail centers on the ground floor.

Care must be taken when selling an office building to an investor when one tenant rents the majority of the space. You must carefully analyze that business's lease to see when it expires, what renewal options are available to the tenant in the lease, whether a renewal option has already been exercised before, and how well the business seems to be doing. If that tenant decides to vacate at the end of its lease, your investor could be faced with a mostly vacant building for an extended period of time.

New tenants in an office building may each want tenant improvements (TIs) made to the space they are renting that are unique to their business. Who pays for these improvements is negotiable and usually dictated by demand for office space and the current state of the economy as well as the amount of vacancy in that particular building. In many cases, if the building owner pays for the tenant improvements, the cost is amortized over the life of the initial lease period. The owner will always put a maximum limit on what the owner will pay, usually stated as a cost-per-net-rentable square foot. At times, office space has become over-built. When this happens, building owners will often give new tenants a certain number of months of free rent. This is also a common incentive given to tenants who lease in new buildings, especially "name" tenants with strong financial backing from a Fortune 500 parent company.

> Each new tenant in an office building may want tenant improvements made to the space they are renting that are unique to their business.

Review Questions

1. You were driving through your specialty area, and you noticed a run-down 12-unit multifamily property. Listings are in high demand right now. What should you do?
   A. go up and talk to the resident manager
   B. put it in your database when you get the chance
   C. take a picture of it, research the true owner's name, and mail him/her the picture with a letter asking if you can help him/her to rehabilitate or sell the property
   D. call the property manager and ask for the owner's contact information

234   *Chapter 20*

2. You have identified 100 neighborhood retail centers in your metro area that you are going to put in your database. All of them are owned by either a corporation or an LLC. What action will you take to secure the name of a true decision maker?
   A. check the local telephone listings
   B. get an ownership list from your favorite title company and then cross-check by corporate name or LLC name on your state's secretary of state website
   C. get the corporation's or LLC's address and then make a personal visit
   D. both B and C answer choices

3. Which of the following is true about the availability of commercial real estate databases?
   A. The local multiple listing service (MLS) has all the currently listed commercial properties in its database.
   B. CoStar is the only available commercial real estate database, and it only has your area.
   C. CoStar and LoopNet are the two major commercial databases available, but LoopNet has been purchased by CoStar and will disappear soon.
   D. Nearly all commercial brokers belong to the local MLS.

4. Which of the following are primary users of small to midsize office buildings?
   A. real estate firms and insurance agencies
   B. investment firms employing 50 or more advisors
   C. pest control companies and chiropractors
   D. both A and C answer choices

5. High-rise office buildings nearly always have what type of tenants on the ground floor?
   A. office
   B. apartments for long-term lease
   C. retail businesses and shops
   D. property management offices for the retail shop owners

Class Discussion Topics

1. Discuss the different needs of a retail client who requires drive-by business and the needs of a big-box store like Home Depot.
2. How important is it to verify the zoning requirements for your client's particular business, cross-checking the current or proposed zoning of a building they have indicated they would like to purchase? Why is it important?
3. Your client owns a law office and practices elder law. He says he needs to be on the second floor. What is the most important thing you will need to be sure is in any office building he occupies, and why?
4. You have a client who wants to make an offer on a 12,000 square foot office building. Currently, 8,000 square feet are occupied by a real estate firm that is on the last year of its lease. What sort of investigation issues should you do?
5. Discuss the different types of leases that are common to office and retail properties, and explain who pays what in each type of lease.

Chapter 21

Retail Shopping Centers

238   *Chapter 21*

Retail shopping centers vary in size from the small strip center of a few thousand square feet to the neighborhood shopping center with 80,000 to well over 100,000 square feet, to huge regional malls with over a million square feet or more. These properties are currently depreciated over a 39-year period.

The small strip center is common in all urban areas and along major routes throughout the United States. The age, condition, visibility, and traffic count of the buildings and the area where they are located usually dictate the amount and nature of rent owners are able to charge and the type of tenant they are able to attract.

An older strip center in a B area may be able to generate only gross leases because of the marginal tenants they are able to attract. These buildings are often occupied by pawn shops, ethnic markets, small cafés or restaurants, auto pink-slip loan businesses, used bookstores, cellular phone companies, and other such businesses. The net profits derived from nearly all these types of businesses often don't allow the business owner (i.e., tenant) to enter into NNN leases. Newer strip retail centers in better areas will often have real estate offices, insurance brokers, opticians, franchise bagel or coffee stores, small restaurants, and other tenants like those in office buildings. Their businesses will usually support the payment of an NNN lease, and these types of leases are much more prevalent in the better-located, newer strip retail centers and neighborhood centers.

Parking can often be marginal at best with strip centers, and though many have ingress/egress easements with the neighboring properties, it is always good business to evaluate the effect of available parking on the tenants' ability to attract customers. Real estate offices in these types of properties can sometimes be problematic because they need a great deal of parking for the sales agents and staff, which may not leave much for the customers and other tenants; however, as more and more real estate

> It is always good business to evaluate the effect of available parking on the tenants' ability to attract customers.

firms are becoming home based, the difficult parking situation so often associated with them is waning. If you help a client invest in a strip center or small neighborhood center that leases to a real estate firm, investigate what stipulations, if any, are in place to restrict where the sales agents may park and how well they are being enforced.

Much as in office buildings, free rent and payment of tenant improvements are inducements used by owners to attract new retail tenants. The amount, if any, paid by owners is dictated by the supply-and-demand curve.

Strip centers are usually financed only to a maximum of 60 to 65% loan-to-value ratio (LTV), and because they are commercial in nature, the 39-year depreciation schedule must be used. Most leases in these centers are for an initial three- to five-year period and sometimes contain a renewal option for five years at a time.

Nearly every retail shopping center has cross-easements with the adjoining properties that allow customers to walk or drive from one center to the next without having to enter the roadway each time. Resurfacing of the parking lot is a major cost associated with a retail shopping center. If it is not done at reasonable intervals, the pavement can start to split, get water under it, and begin to crumble. A "slurry coat" can be applied every few years accompanied by a restriping of the parking spaces. (A slurry coat is a coat of liquid asphalt/tar that is sprayed over the existing asphalt to seal it from water penetration.) Some retail leases call for the tenants to pay into a parking lot maintenance fund. This money is supposed to be used to maintain the parking lot, but it is usually

240   *Chapter 21*

credited through escrow from one owner to the next and is actually used only when it is absolutely necessary and, far too often, well after it is critically necessary.

> Resurfacing of the parking lot is a major cost associated with a retail shopping center.

"Hydrocarbon" businesses are gas stations, oil-changing businesses, and any other such businesses that use oil fuel in any form. Hydrocarbon businesses are normally found in the neighborhood shopping centers and regional malls. It is rare that a strip center will have a business with hydrocarbons on-site, but if you are involved in representing someone in the sale or purchase of a retail center that has hydrocarbons, be sure to see that at least a Phase 1 Environmental Site Assessment is ordered in a timely manner because this report will certainly be a lender requirement if your investor is financing the acquisition. Three phases of environmental reports may apply to any property where hydrocarbons or other contaminants have been present:

- *Phase 1 environmental report.* This is a record check of the local building department, health department, or other government agency to see if there has been any cease-and-desist order made or any demand to clean up a hydrocarbon spill.

- *Phase 2 environmental report.* This is an on-site inspection of the business using hydrocarbons and the surrounding area to see if any visible spills or storage tank leakage has taken place. It is usually conducted or overseen by a representative from the Environmental Protection Agency of the federal government.

- *Phase 3 environmental report.* This report requires boring test holes or small wells and obtaining soil samples at various spots around the affected property to see if any of the samples contain traces of hydrocarbons. Many lenders will make a Phase 2 environmental report a minimum requirement if there are any hydrocarbon businesses on the premises they are being asked to finance. If the property was ever foreclosed on by the lender, who then became the owner, that lender could be made to pay for any environmental cleanup, which can cost from $300,000 to well over $1 million. The main issue has been gas stations with leaking gasoline storage tanks.

Like office buildings, retail shopping centers house businesses. That makes them and the tenants in them subject to the ups and downs of the economy; so when you are representing someone in the marketing or purchase of a retail shopping center, be sensitive to the current state of the national, state, and local economies, given that all may affect the value of the property.

Neighborhood retail shopping centers are larger than strip centers and usually contain several acres of land. Many have an "anchor tenant" that adds value to the center because of its financial stability and its ability to attract customers to the center for the other businesses. Good examples of anchor tenants would be Costco, Wal-Mart, Safeway, Walgreens, or any other big-name commercial business that attracts a lot of customers. A center can also be "shadow anchored" by a major tenant; that is, the property immediately next to the center has a major tenant, and it is an easy walk to the "shadowed" retail center.

> Neighborhood retail shopping centers are larger than strip centers and usually contain several acres of land.

Neighborhood retail centers often have excellent restaurants, fast-food outlets such as Burger King or McDonald's, and businesses

242   *Chapter 21*

that play to customers on a higher financial level. The larger ones are often anchored by an anchor tenant such as Home Depot, Lowe's, Costco, Target, or some other major retailer. Many also have a gas station on-site, so, again, be very careful.

The regional malls are usually anchored by several major retailers such as J.C. Penney, Sears, Robinsons-May, Macy's, Banana Republic, or any number of other highly successful retailers. There are often several jewelry stores in a regional mall. One note of caution: There has been a movement of consolidation among some retailers in recent years, and if two or more major retail stores, such as Robinsons-May and Macy's (both are owned by Federated), are tenants in the same mall, the mall owners could be in for a vacancy if they combine operations, as happened in the Tucson Mall in Tucson, Arizona, several years ago. Regional malls are currently closing at a rate of several thousand a year all across America. Several have been turned into college campuses while others have converted the empty "big-box" store into several smaller online shopping merchandise pickup points. People's shopping habits have changed drastically. The Internet has literally changed the way a large portion of the public shops now, and the big-box retail stores have seen a sharp downturn in the number of customers who actually come in to shop.

Because of the large parking lots and security issues, the regional malls are more vulnerable to litigation from customers who have been assaulted or had their car stolen, so if you are involved in the brokerage of one of these malls, be sure to see what type of security patrols are in place and check with the local law enforcement agencies to see what, if any, problems have occurred in the past two or three years. This should always be a part of your due diligence work.

Many of the leases signed by the major retailers are long term in nature, with many lasting 25 to 30 years. An escalation clause related to the Consumer Price Index is still sometimes in place, usually with a cap of 3 to 5% annually; however, most of these leases are currently tying rent increases to a fixed percentage of the then-existing lease amount. These types of leases are very lengthy and detailed, and they should always be reviewed by the buyer's attorney and CPA. Most neighborhood retail centers and all regional malls have leases that allow the major tenants a rent abatement or the right to abandon their lease in the event another major tenant leaves the premises.

Review Questions

1. A strip center on a very busy street has inadequate parking. What detrimental issues may come into play?
   A. inability to rent vacant units
   B. lower value
   C. lower rents
   D. all of the answer choices

2. Which of the following statements is true of a neighborhood retail center?
   A. Parking lot maintenance is a minor part of ongoing maintenance.
   B. A slurry coat every few years will extend the life of a parking lot.
   C. Parking lot maintenance is a capital improvement, not maintenance.
   D. A slurry coat has no effect on the life of a parking lot.

244 *Chapter 21*

3. Your client is investing in a neighborhood retail center that has a gas station on the premises. What language should your purchase agreement contain?
   A. a contingency of the buyer's verbal approval of an economic report on the gas station operation
   B. the requirement that the seller supply your buyer with a new Phase 1 environmental report, or up to a Phase 3 environmental report if required by the buyer's lender
   C. a contingency that the buyer be allowed access to the gas station for the buyer's personal walk-through inspection and approval
   D. no specific language required because the seller's agent told you the gas station is "clean"

4. You are showing your buyer a neighborhood retail center that has an Oil Changers business on a front pad of the center. As you walk through it with your buyer, you see a lot of oil stains on the pavement and on a dirt area at the rear of the property. How should you advise your buyer?
   A. point out these issues and explain the possibilities of contamination
   B. do nothing because the lender will surely find out about it and make sure the seller fixes it
   C. notify the Environmental Protection Agency
   D. notify the local authorities because this is a violation of the law

5. Which of the following would be considered an anchor tenant in a regional shopping center?
   A. locally owned restaurant that has been in business for two years
   B. carpet company that has five offices in town
   C. J.C. Penney department store
   D. Nico's Taco Shop

Class Discussion Topics

1. You have sold a $2.5-million strip center to a client. When you review the leases, you find that nearly all of them either have expired or will expire in a matter of months. How should you advise your client?

2. You are showing a strip center to your client, and the parking lot is full. Your client is impressed. You note that three-fourths of the property is leased by a large real estate company's branch office. What would be the most important thing you would want to review, and why?

3. Jerry Liu has sold a neighborhood retail center that has a gas station on it. The Chevron signs are still in place, but the station is closed and surrounded by a chicken-wire fence. The listing says nothing about the station. What questions should Jerry ask of the listing agent?

4. Juliet Nance showed a regional mall to her client, and they both noted that a major department store has vacated. Juliet read in the *Wall Street Journal* that Best Buy is looking for a large space in a regional mall in that area. What actions should Juliet take?

5. You sold an $8.750-million neighborhood retail center with a strong national anchor tenant. When you review the anchor tenant's lease, you see that the anchor tenant still has 17 years remaining on its lease, and there is no escalator clause. What effect does this have on the present and future value of the center, and what advice would you give to your client?

Chapter 22

Self-Storage Facilities

248   *Chapter 22*

Mini storage facilities, or self-storage facilities, as they are referred to now, are a very different breed of real estate investment. They are not the sexiest income-producing properties by any means, but properly managed, self-storage facilities are unequaled as cash cows. They have a true operating expense ratio of approximately 19 to 24% of gross scheduled income, as compared with 30 to 36% for multifamily properties.

> They are not the sexiest income-producing properties by any means, but properly managed, self-storage facilities are unequaled as cash cows.

Self-storage facilities can consist of a small plot of land with fewer than 30 units to several acres containing several hundred units with two-story air-conditioned buildings. They are often located near mobile home parks and large residential subdivisions because their residents' need for additional storage makes them target tenants. Many facilities derive additional income from truck or trailer rentals and the sale of moving boxes and related goods. Some facilities are a combination of self-storage and boat/recreational vehicle storage.

There are three main types of construction of self-storage facilities: concrete block walls with sloped tar-and-gravel roofs and metal doors, all-metal construction, and wood frame/stucco with a hip roof covered in asphalt shingles.

Regardless of the type of construction, care must be taken to evaluate the soil before beginning construction. Heavy clay soil expands when it gets wet, and if the facility's foundation is not prepared properly, every time it rains the soil under the units will expand unevenly and the garage entry doors to the units won't open because the door tracks will be thrown out of alignment. You

Self-Storage Facilities **249**

may avoid this problem by requiring the construction of "floating foundations," where the perimeter foundation is poured and then approximately 2 feet of soil is removed from the interior and replaced with gravel and nonexpansive dirt that is compacted to 94%. A floating foundation is poured over the compacted nonexpansive soil, and the buildings are then built on the floating foundation, which rises and falls evenly.

Concrete block construction is labor intensive to build but easily maintained thereafter. Most older concrete block facilities have sloped tar-and-gravel roofs that need to be maintained on a regular basis; however, for several years now, composition-shingle roofs have been the norm. When performing an income/expense analysis on this type of facility, be sure to allow for annual maintenance costs and a reserve fund to allow for roof replacement at regular intervals of 10 to 15 years, depending on the type of roof and where the facility is located.

Metal buildings are the least expensive to construct, but they can be more of a maintenance challenge, depending on the type and quality of construction. For instance, they usually have pitched metal roofs that are fastened together with pop-rivets at the roof apex. To avoid leaking, plastic grommets are used in conjunction with the pop-rivet installation. If the roof apex is not protected from the elements, the sun will eventually cause the grommets to become so brittle that they will crack and come apart, causing massive roof leaks. Replacing them can be a maintenance nightmare. In better-quality metal construction, a metal cap that runs the entire length of each building is placed over the rivets and snapped in place. This cap acts as a barrier to both sun and water and effectively solves the leak situation. Not all types of metal construction can be retrofitted with a cap system, so be sure to investigate this issue during your due diligence period if you are representing a property with a building that has this type of construction.

250   Chapter 22

Wood-frame/stucco construction with a normal hip roof that slopes down on each side has become very popular in the last 20 years. It is easy to construct and reasonably easy to maintain. Exterior maintenance reserves will be for painting and roof replacement every so often, but this roof type is usually much more adaptable than tar and gravel and will not have to be repaired as often. This type of construction is most often found in two-story facilities. A two-story facility will, out of necessity, include an elevator. Elevator maintenance will increase operating expenses somewhat, so be careful to check elevator maintenance costs in your area.

Until about 1980, the main type of security at a self-storage facility was when the resident manager closed and locked the gate at night and let the guard dogs out. Theft deterrence and security have become an issue with self-storage facilities, and closed-circuit television systems that monitor an entire facility are routine now. All but the smallest facilities have an on-site apartment where a resident manager lives. The ideal candidate for this position is often a retired husband-wife team who get free rent and a salary in return for overseeing the operation. They act as night guards and run the day-to-day operation, which includes collecting rents, showing and renting units, handling notices and on-site auctions of personal property left by people who don't pay or who abandon property on the site, and engaging in some level of recordkeeping and banking. An intense interview and thorough background check on any new management candidate is the rule, including checking all references!

Self-storage facilities have often been constructed on land purchased by a developer who wants to derive an income from the property while he/she waits for urban spread to reach the property, which will make it much more valuable for residential development.

Location is extremely important when considering a self-storage acquisition or new build. You must be certain that the site location is not vulnerable to someone building a new facility nearer to your target market than your site is, because this may cause many of your tenants to vacate and move to the newer facility, and your target market will probably opt to rent at the newer, closer facility.

> You must be certain that the site location is not vulnerable to someone building a new facility nearer to your target market than your site is.

If you ever want to spend a few days in the company of a large group of very low-key multimillionaires, attend the annual self-storage owners' convention. They are a most impressive group!

Self-storage developments are also depreciated over a 39-year period.

Review Questions

1. Self-storage properties are known for which of the following?
   A. higher operating expenses than most other investments
   B. lower operating expenses than most other investments
   C. operating expenses that are about the same as most other investments
   D. lower operating expenses except for roof issues

252 *Chapter 22*

2. Which of the following statements is NOT true about self-storage facilities?
   A. Self-storage facility owners like to be located near large mobile home parks.
   B. Large residential subdivisions are a desired target market.
   C. A potential development site zoned for self-storage and nearer to your target market poses a potential threat.
   D. none of the answer choices; all of them are true

3. The easiest type of self-storage construction to maintain is which of the following?
   A. concrete block construction with a pitched composition-shingle roof
   B. all-metal construction
   C. wood-frame/stucco construction
   D. both A and B answer choices

4. Which of the following is an additional revenue source for self-storage facilities?
   A. the sale of moving boxes and related materials
   B. recreational vehicle and/or boat storage
   C. rental income from the resident managers
   D. both A and B answer choices

5. When constructing a self-storage facility, care must be taken to investigate which of the following?
   A. type of soil for expansive clay
   B. which type of construction is allowed by local ordinances
   C. height limitations
   D. all of the answer choices

Self-Storage Facilities   253

Class Discussion Topics

1. Describe the steps in constructing a self-storage facility with floating foundations, and explain why they are sometimes necessary.
2. You represent a buyer in the purchase of a $4-million self-storage facility. It is metal construction and 27 years old. What issues will be important inspection points, and why?
3. Discuss the additional revenue sources available to self-storage facilities, and explain the potential positive and negative issues associated with each one.
4. Name the different types of theft deterrence available to self-storage facilities, and tell the class how effective each one may be.
5. On-site resident managers are often mature couples who are retired. Discuss what would be relevant questions to ask interviewees to see if they are a good fit for the position without engaging in age discrimination.

Chapter 23

Single-Tenant NNN-Leased Investments

256   *Chapter 23*

Single-tenant NNN-leased investments are often called "coupon clippers" because the owner has virtually no management duties or obligations except to cash the rent check. These investments include fast-food restaurants such as McDonald's and Burger King, auto care firms such as Midas Muffler shops and Jiffy Lube, Walgreens and other major drug stores, bank branch offices, major supermarkets such as Safeway, and major chain retailers such as Target, PetSmart, K-Mart, and others. Many of the larger types of these investments are anchor tenants in large neighborhood shopping centers, though some, such as the drug stores and banks, are usually stand-alone.

> Single-tenant NNN-leased investments are often called "coupon clippers."

The tenant reimburses the owner for virtually all operating costs incurred in connection with the property, and the tenants each pay their own utilities and janitorial services. With anchor tenants and major franchise properties, the rent is usually paid or guaranteed by the parent company, which is often a Fortune 500 company or a highly successful owner of a regional franchise.

The leases are usually for a long period of time—some as long as 25 to 30 years. Because of the long term, the lease almost always contains an escalator clause that adjusts the rent periodically to keep up with inflation. The increases are sometimes tied to the Consumer Price Index (CPI), a measure of the cost of living, or are a fixed percentage of the then-existing rent, and most are capped at 3 to 5% annually.

There is a tax issue with NNN-leased investments that you should always have your clients investigate with their CPA or tax attorney before making this type of investment. Because owners have

Single-Tenant NNN-Leased Investments **257**

virtually no ongoing management duties and don't meet the 750-hour (self-management) annual rule, they may not be eligible to take a depreciation allowance from the property.

When helping a client invest in these types of properties, as part of your due diligence you need to examine the lease as well as the condition of the area, the buildings, and the retail center.

- *Have you carefully reviewed the lease?*

    1. How much time is remaining on the lease?

    2. Are there any options to renew?

    3. How likely is it that the tenant will renew?

    4. Is there an escalator clause?

    5. Is it a true NNN lease?

    6. Is there a major net worth guarantor on the lease?

    7. Who pays for roof and parking lot maintenance?

- *What is the condition and status of the area?*

    1. Is the area building, declining, or staying the same? If, for instance, you are showing your client a supermarket that is in the last six years of a 30-year lease in an older retail center, and a new center is being built a few blocks away that will include a major competitor supermarket, the tenant in the property you are showing to your client may be considering closing that operation at the end of the current lease. That would leave your client with the possibility of a huge loan payment and no income to pay it.

    2. What is the crime rate in the area?

258   *Chapter 23*

- *What is the condition of the building itself and the retail center it is in?*

    1. While it is true the tenants must maintain the building, what kind of a job are they doing?

    2. Is there any sign of deferred maintenance?

    3. Does the property show signs of functional obsolescence that would be very expensive or impossible to cure?

    4. If the property is in a retail center, how well is the center being maintained?

> If the property is in a retail center, how well is the center being maintained?

One final note of caution: Any single-user investment property may, at some time, be subjected to an extended vacancy if the property no longer serves the existing tenant at or near the end of the lease. It is therefore imperative that you caution any investor you work with who is considering ownership of single-user investment property of that possibility and suggest that the investor maintain a larger-than-normal financial reserve. These funds need to be reasonably accessible, and receiving the highest return on them while they exist may be best accomplished by a series of bank certificates of deposit (CDs), the first one maturing in 30 days, the second in 60 days, and so on, until the investor's comfort level is reached. Then as the first CD matures, it should be reinvested at the same duration period as the very last one. This will eventually end up with the investor holding a number of long-term CDs that are maturing every 30 days and are at maximum bank interest rates.

Single-Tenant NNN-Leased Investments 259

Review Questions

1. Which of the following must the owner of a NNN-leased investment pay?

   A. Owner pays all operating expenses except the tenants' janitorial and utility expenses and is reimbursed by the tenants each month.

   B. Tenants pay all operating expenses directly to vendors and taxing agency.

   C. Owner pays only taxes and insurance. (The tenants pay the rest.)

   D. Owner pays all the bills, including for the tenants' utilities and janitorial services. (The tenants will reimburse for all of them.)

2. What are two important nontenant issues to consider when investing in a single-user NNN-leased property?

   A. the area's status (declining, stable, or improving) and the tenants' financial statements

   B. the area's status and the competition for tenants from newer properties nearby

   C. the area's status and the likelihood of tenant vacancies

   D. nearby competition from like-kind tenants and how often the tenant has been late paying the rent

3. Your client is considering making an offer on a major bank branch facility with full knowledge that the bank is vacating at the end of its lease in a few months. Which of the following could result in an extended vacancy?

   A. functional obsolescence that can be cured

   B. economic and potential incurable functional obsolescence resulting from the closure of several bank branches in the general area

   C. inability to retain and use the tenant's security deposit

   D. none of the answer choices

260   *Chapter 23*

4. Which of the following statements is NOT true?
   A. The owner of a NNN-leased property who does not meet the 750-hour-per-year self-management rule may use only a 39-year depreciation schedule.
   B. The owner of a NNN-leased property who meets the 750-hour-per-year rule may use only a 27.5-year depreciation schedule.
   C. The owner of a NNN-leased property may never take a depreciation allowance deduction on his/her tax return.
   D. all of the answer choices

5. Which of the following NNN-leased properties would probably sell at the highest capitalization rate?
   A. building occupied by a branch office of a large, locally owned real estate firm in the process of consolidating offices
   B. CVS Pharmacy located in a well-run neighborhood retail center
   C. McDonald's restaurant owned by the parent company
   D. office building completely leased to the Bear Stearns Investment firm with 22 years remaining on the lease

Class Discussion Topics

1. What is the greatest risk of owning a single-tenant NNN-leased property, and why?
2. Assuming that the owner of a NNN-leased investment property meets the 750-hour-per-year self-management rule, is he/she eligible for a depreciation deduction on his/her tax returns, and if so, which schedule must the owner use?
3. You are representing a client in the purchase of a Burger King restaurant. Name and discuss the seven issues in the lease that must be carefully reviewed.

Single-Tenant NNN-Leased Investments 261

4. Explain why an escalator clause is found in virtually all commercial leases, and why the annual CPI increase is seldom used today. What would be the effect on the value of a long-term NNN-leased property if the lease did not contain an escalator clause?

5. You are representing a client who likes to buy run-down strip centers in marginal areas, rehabilitate and re-lease them, and then sell them. In what parts of town will you primarily be operating, and what are some of the issues you should be particularly aware of?

Chapter 24

Land Brokerage

264   *Chapter 24*

Land brokerage has one of the highest litigation rates against brokers of any type of commercial brokerage. It is no place for the unschooled to dally, and it is one of the areas of commercial brokerage most scrutinized by the Department of Real Estate.

> Land brokerage has one of the highest litigation rates against brokers of any type of commercial brokerage.

Land brokerage includes selling subdivided lots in existing subdivisions where homes have already been built, newly subdivided lots that are being sold to the public or to builders by a developer, the sale of large estate-type acreage to custom-home builders or homeowners, and the sale of raw land to commercial property developers as well as residential developers. The sale of ranches and farms is somewhat different because it also entails the sale of an existing business with the land, and possibly a crop that is not ready to harvest. Ranch-and-farm brokerage is an even more specialized type of land sales and should be conducted only by highly experienced professionals.

Let's take a look at each type of brokerage.

Subdivided Lots in Existing Subdivisions

Brokerage of subdivided lots in existing subdivisions is the safest type of land sale, especially if there are already several homes built around the lot you are trying to sell. The reasons it is safer are as follows:

- It is easier to verify the existence and exact location of all utilities, including natural gas, electricity, water, sewer, and trash removal.

- It is easier to verify the existence of sewer lines and hookup capability or to obtain existing percolation tests of adjoining properties if an on-site waste treatment system such as a septic system is needed. Properties built in areas that need a septic system but fail a percolation test must have an on-site self-contained septic system installed, and these are very expensive.

- Boundary lines are easier to determine.

- The existence of any flood zones or special study zones, such as seismic study zones or earthquake zones in California, is easier to determine.

- The availability of crime and fire prevention, as well as who is responsible for it, is easier to determine.

- There are often more recent comparable sales to use in determining the property value.

- If this is the first sale of this property to the public, a Final Public Report may be needed.

Newly Subdivided Land Being Sold to the Public or to Builders

The brokerage of newly subdivided land that is being sold to the public or to builders involves the use and proper issuance of many items not used in resale land brokerage. Some of these are as follows:

- *Commissioner's Preliminary Subdivision Public Report.* In most states, a developer can take a reservation on a lot from the public and can take a refundable deposit. The buyer must

266   *Chapter 24*

acknowledge receipt of a Preliminary Subdivision Public Report, and the reservation is cancelable by either party until the buyer is issued a Final Subdivision Public Report, at which time the sale is finalized and the buyer's deposit becomes nonrefundable.

- *Final Subdivision Public Report.* Once a subdivision is fully approved by the Department of Real Estate, a Final Subdivision Public Report will be issued. Anyone who entered into a reservation must either sign for the Final Subdivision Public Report and make the deposit nonrefundable at that time or withdraw from the reservation and receive the deposit back. All new sales are binding at that time and must include the buyer's signed receipt for the Final Subdivision Public Report.

> Once a subdivision is fully approved by the Department of Real Estate, a Final Subdivision Public Report will be issued.

- *rights of rescission time limits.* Land subdivisions are often subject to long and stringent time periods for the buyers to reconsider and cancel the purchase. California, for instance, has a 10-day right of rescission for new subdivision land sales.

- *trust fund handling of customer deposits.* It is common for a developer to have language in the purchase agreement he/she is using that alerts the buyer that the developer is placing the buyer's deposit into the developer's business account and not into a neutral escrow account. This could place the buyer's deposit in jeopardy if the developer files for bankruptcy protection.

Land Brokerage 267

- *due diligence periods (also called feasibility study periods).* Builders who purchase lots in bulk from a subdivider almost always want a "feasibility study" or "due diligence" period included in their purchase or option agreement. The timing of these periods can vary from a few weeks to several months and allows the builder/buyer time to assess the strength or weakness of the current market and the anticipated market conditions when he/she is able to bring a finished home to the market. Your job as an agent for the builder would be to obtain information about what price-range home would be optimal to build on the land the builder is acquiring and what the anticipated absorption rate would be (i.e., how fast the builder's product would be purchased by the public).

As the agent for the developer, you will have the job of getting as high a price per lot from the builders and individual buyers as possible, with the fewest concessions possible. You may be asked to help the developer determine the optimum lot premium that should be charged for each lot in the subdivision he/she is developing. You may also be asked to plan a complete marketing and advertising campaign, including newsprint, websites, marketing brochures, and direct mailing campaigns.

The developer often relies on his/her real estate professional to obtain comparable sales information on similar land transactions so that the developer can properly plan his/her best pricing strategy and optimize his/her profit from the venture.

> The developer often relies on his/her real estate agent to obtain comparable sales information on similar land transactions.

268   *Chapter 24*

Sale of Large Estate-Type Acreage to Custom-Home Builders or Homeowners

The sale of large estate-type acreage to custom-home builders or homeowners can often be conducted in such a manner that the issuance of a Final Subdivision Public Report is not needed. You must be careful to see that any subdivision of land in this manner is a legitimate one and not a "wildcat" subdivision as defined by the Department of Real Estate in your state. For instance, in Arizona, any land subdivision of five or fewer parcels is exempt from a public report, whereas California's threshold is six or fewer parcels. Commissioner's Preliminary and Final Public Reports take a lot of time and cost a lot of money, so some developers are tempted to do a wildcat subdivision to avoid the time and expense.

I was recently made aware of a situation where a newer agent was listing a man's 10-acre parcel that he had subdivided into five 2-acre parcels. The agent was walking the property with the seller and an appraiser and met the owner of the adjacent 10-acre parcel, which he had just acquired as well. The agent asked him if he would consider selling his five 2-acre parcels, and he agreed. When the listings were reviewed by the branch manager, he became suspicious and investigated further, at which time he found that this was, indeed, a wildcat subdivision of a 20-acre parcel that was split into two 10-acre parcels and then split again into five 2-acre parcels each. He cancelled the listing and notified the Department of Real Estate, as he was supposed to do.

The Department of Real Estate levied a heavy fine against each property owner and issued a cease-and-desist order, stopping the sale, and it notified both owners that they could not sell the land for at least two years. The designated broker of the firm was fined $4,000 because the agent took the listings; the branch manager

Land Brokerage   269

was fined $2,000 because the agent took the listings; the agent was fined $20,000 and almost had her license suspended. As you can see, it is easy to become entangled in something very unpleasant if you are not familiar with what you are doing in land sales.

Your job as a builder's representative is to help assess the value of each parcel acquired by your builder client and the optimum price, style, and size of the home that can be built on each one. An assessment of the current market and the anticipated strength or weakness of the market when the finished home is placed for sale is also among your duties. This price analysis is critical to the success of the project because it allows the builder or developer to maximize profits by not overpaying for the land.

Some builders of these types of homes will rely heavily on their agents for staging and decorating advice; others will use the services of a professional decorator, especially if model homes are involved.

Sale of Raw Land to Developers

The sale of raw land to developers is an area of land sales that probably has the highest legal exposure for a real estate professional. This is where you, as an agent, are finding and presenting large parcels of undeveloped land to developers and builders.

Many issues need to be investigated during the due diligence period. Some states maintain that you, as the agent for the developer, are primarily responsible for proper investigation of material facts regarding the proposed land purchase on behalf of your client. Some states maintain that the client is primarily responsible for the investigation of material facts and that you, as the agent, are secondarily responsible. Either way, you will need to become keenly aware of any land-related issues that could

270   *Chapter 24*

affect the proposed purchase your client is about to make. Zoning, special-study (earthquake) zones, flood zones, known "brownfields" or areas of contamination, building height or size restrictions, easements, minimum-lot-size concerns, building setback ordinances, and sewer capacity availability are just a few of the issues you will need to be aware of. Failure to investigate even one of these can result in your client purchasing land that he/she cannot develop as planned, and your client could take a huge loss or lose a large earnest money deposit.

> Failure to investigate even one of these can result in your client's purchasing land that he/she cannot develop as planned.

Arizona places the primary responsibility on the client but holds the agent to a high degree of backup responsibility. A case happened not so long ago where a developer-client made an offer to purchase over 130 acres for residential development. He was very egotistical, and when the agent reminded him to check on the sewer capacity, he told the agent that he knew what he was doing and had a whole team to do that stuff. Fortunately, the agent faxed the developer the paperwork to fill out and submit to the county to find out about sewer capacity. The client initialed each page and faxed it back. Well after the expiration of the due diligence period, the developer became aware that there was no sewer capacity, and he cancelled the sale. He threatened to sue the agent, broker, and seller for "willful nondisclosure" and fraud if his $50,000 deposit was not returned. When his attorney was presented with the county paperwork that was sent to and initialed by the developer, he redirected his wrath at the seller for failure to disclose the lack of sewer capacity (the seller had known it and hadn't disclosed it), and he got his deposit back. Having "provable" evidence of diligence on the agent's part by faxing the paperwork and getting it back saved the agent and brokerage firm many thousands of dollars in defense fees; nonetheless, both he and his company had to pay attorney fees to make the situation go away. The entire matter could have been avoided, however, had the agent checked on the sewer capacity himself.

Another issue is that when a process server serves you with a summons and complaint (in essence, a lawsuit), it can and often does put you mentally out of business, which can cost you thousands of dollars in commissions that you would have earned through other clients. So be very careful!

Anyone who is sincerely interested in specializing in land brokerage is well advised to start with a mentor for the first few transactions and take course offerings in land sales. The REALTORS® Land Institute offers a course of study leading to the RLI professional designation.

Review Questions

1. Selling lots in a subdivided development will require you to know about which of the following?
   A. location and proximity of the electrical hookup and availability of natural gas, and its location and proximity
   B. availability of a public sewer system and its location and proximity
   C. availability, location, and proximity of water service
   D. all of the answer choices

272   *Chapter 24*

2. A woman calls to ask you to list her five-parcel subdivision. Your state requires a Final Subdivision Public Report for parcel splits of six or more parcels. What action(s) must you take before listing the property?

   A. walk the property to check for utilities placement
   B. ask if she purchased the land recently from someone for whom it was part of another five-parcel subdivision
   C. contact the Department of Real Estate to verify her story, and do not list the property if it was part of a previous five-parcel split, and ask your broker to contact the Department of Real Estate about the matter
   D. both B and C answer choices

3. In Arizona, when selling raw land to a client, who is primarily liable for all the due diligence issues that must be investigated and verified, and who is secondarily liable?

   A. The client is primarily liable, and the real estate agent is secondarily liable.
   B. The agent is primarily liable, and the client is secondarily liable.
   C. The client assumes all the liability for due diligence.
   D. The agent and the client are equally liable for proper due diligence.

4. The sale of which type of land has the highest level of litigation against real estate brokers?

   A. lots in an existing subdivision
   B. newly subdivided land to developers and builders
   C. raw land
   D. multi-acre sites to luxury-home builders

5. Which of the following statements is NOT true?
   A. A developer may put the buyer's earnest money in his/her general business account.
   B. A developer is not required to put the buyer's earnest money deposit in an interest-bearing trust account within three days after he/she receives it.
   C. A developer may put the buyer's earnest money deposit in his business trust account.
   D. A developer may not take an earnest money deposit until he/she starts construction on the buyer's new home.

Class Discussion Topics

1. Discuss why it is recommended that an agent new to land sales work with a mentor for a period of time, and indicate what the results of not doing so may be.
2. A client tells you he wants to make an offer on a 37-acre parcel to build luxury homes on the land. Discuss what your due diligence investigations would cover, and tell why each is important.
3. You are selling lots in a newly subdivided 103-acre subdivision that has an approved Preliminary Subdivision Public Report. Describe the step-by-step process you would go through in selling a lot to a young couple who want to purchase a new home.
4. Describe the many due diligence issues you need to investigate for a client who is buying a very large parcel of land to build an upscale residential subdivision.
5. During the course of a land purchase, you give reminders, warnings, and suggestions in conversations with your client and have conversations with the building and zoning department, the planning commission, the title company, subcontractors, and others. Which of these conversations should be memorialized in writing and copied in some manner and sent to your client? Which ones should be copied and placed in your escrow file?

Chapter 25

Mobile Home Parks

276   *Chapter 25*

Mobile home parks may consist of a few to several acres of land that have been developed with streets that have cement pads on either side to accommodate mobile homes. The mobile homes may be park owned and rented to tenants, or they may be tenant owned, with the tenants paying a space rental for the pad and surrounding area they rent. Mobile home parks can usually be financed to approximately 60 to 65% of appraised value.

Most mobile home parks have amenities available for use by the tenants. The number and type of amenities will usually vary according to the economic stature of the community and neighborhood where they are located and may include a swimming pool, clubhouse, exercise room, or vending machines. A covered, off-street vehicle parking pad alongside each unit is usually provided.

> The number and type of amenities will usually vary according to the economic stature of the community and neighborhood where they are located.

Mobile home parks have varying levels of quality. Some of the factors that define the quality of a mobile home park are described here.

Ratio of Single-Wide to Double-Wide Units

A mobile home park that has many or mostly single-wide units will usually have a higher vacancy rate than a park that has all or mostly double-wide units. The reason is that the owner of a single-wide unit can easily hook it up to a truck or sports utility vehicle and move it to another park, leaving the park owner with a vacant pad, whereas the owner of a double-wide unit must have the unit split in two and hauled to another location on two flatbed trucks followed by a vehicle bearing a Wide Load sign behind them. This is expensive to do, and so if the owner of a double-wide mobile home wishes to move, he/she will almost always sell the unit and purchase a new one at the new destination. The effect of this on the park owner is that the space is always rented. Real estate professionals are allowed to sell mobile homes as long as the homes are permanently affixed to the land. This is usually accomplished by setting the homes on a perimeter foundation.

Location

Parks that are mostly or totally single-wide in nature are most often found in areas that are on the lower end of the socioeconomic scale in any given community because they afford relatively inexpensive shelter. Parks that tend to have mostly or all double-wide units are usually found in more upscale areas of a community. There are many absolutely beautiful parks with a large number of amenities and long-term tenants across the country. The capitalization rate for a park of this nature will be lower (meaning a higher relative value) than for a mostly single-wide park.

Amenities

Whereas there are few, if any, amenities in a single-wide park because the tenants aren't seeking them, they become an important drawing card for tenants in double-wide parks because these individuals are often retired and are looking for social interaction with other people to fill their time. A central clubhouse, swimming pool, and spa or exercise room are all sought-after features.

> You should advise the client to have the condition of any park-owned units checked thoroughly by an inspector who is familiar with mobile home construction.

Condition of Park-Owned Units

If you, as an agent, are representing an investor in the purchase of a mobile home park, you should advise the client to have the condition of any park-owned units checked thoroughly by an inspector who is familiar with mobile home construction. The inspector must be especially diligent in checking the plumbing because many mobile homes built in the 1980s and early 1990s were constructed with polybutylene plastic plumbing that is highly prone to cracking at the joints and leaking.

Common-Area Issues

In evaluating a mobile home park, you should be careful to look over the entire property. Consider the following common-area issues:

1. Pay attention to maintenance and safety matters.

   - Are the streets and common areas maintained properly?

   - Are roads properly surfaced and free of ruts, dips, and cracks?

   - Are the lawns mowed and trimmed?

   - Are the common buildings painted and in good repair?

   - Are the pool and spa maintained properly, and are there child safety barriers in place?

   - Are the units required to have skirts and be on blocks or jacks?

   - Are the lots wide enough to accommodate a carport?

Mobile Home Parks   279

- What security measures are in place for the park?

- What is the park's proximity to shopping, schools, public transportation, and medical facilities?

2. Meet the on-site managers and interview them; look over their quarters if possible.

   - Are they neat and orderly?

   - Do they seem sharp and in touch with what is going on around the park?

   - If you see any deferred maintenance, ask the managers about why it exists. An interview of this type will tell you much about how well run the park is.

3. Thoroughly review the park owner's accounting records for the past two years. Pay special attention to the following:

   - Total income:

     a. What was the total income received from all sources during the past two years and the year to date?

     b. Does the income show a seasonal trend? Some parks have tenancies that are seasonal in nature. If this is the case, your investor needs to know that he/she will need to use excess reserves carefully to see the operation through the off-season.

   - Total expenses:

     a. Look for any excessive or unusual expenses. Ask what they were for or why they were made if the reason is not clear. Many income property owners pay

280   *Chapter 25*

themselves "perks" for tax reasons that need to be added back into income because they are personal in nature, such as car payments and travel expenses.

b. Compare the property taxes for the two years to see the amount of annual increase, if any.

c. Look for a pattern of routine maintenance expenditures, for both the rental units and the general buildings and common area. This includes painting, lawn and garden care, tree trimming, road maintenance, janitorial services and/or supplies, and pool/spa maintenance and supplies.

d. Calculate the vacancy factor, both in dollars and as a percentage of gross rents. See if it matches any marketing brochure you have received.

One last thing: If you are going to specialize in mobile home parks, get to know a local bank or other lender that will finance them, take the loan officer to lunch, and ask him/her to explain the lending programs they currently have for mobile home parks. Also ask about financing for the individual units in the parks. Take good notes, and keep the information handy! Be sure to set yourself apart from the crowd by sending the loan officer a handwritten thank-you note in a timely manner.

Review Questions

1. A mobile home park in an older, economically depressed part of town would probably include which of the following amenities?
   A. swimming pool
   B. fitness center
   C. horseshoe pit
   D. large meeting hall with a kitchen

Mobile Home Parks 281

2. Which of the following statements about mobile home parks is true?
   A. Their pads usually include a covered pad for vehicle parking.
   B. Each pad usually has a one-car garage.
   C. Their pads do not generally have off-street parking.
   D. They offer off-street parking for an additional fee.

3. Which of the following about the effect of location on the value of a mobile home park is true?
   A. The location has nothing to do with a park's value.
   B. The location has a little to do with a park's value.
   C. The location is of paramount importance in determining a park's value.
   D. The location is important, but not as important as the amenities offered.

4. In which type of mobile home park are the homeowners likely to be more mobile?
   A. all-double-wide park
   B. park where 70% of homes are single-wide
   C. park where 25% of homes are single-wide
   D. all-single-wide park

5. You have decided to specialize in B and C area mobile home park brokerage. Besides training and for a time working with a mentor, you should get to know which very important person(s)?
   A. one or more local bankers who make mobile home park loans
   B. long-time tenants in several of the parks you will add to your database
   C. off-site management companies that manage upscale mobile home parks
   D. the contact person at Zillow

282   *Chapter 25*

Class Discussion Topics

1. You have decided to specialize in upscale mobile home parks. You have been mailing to park owners for five months, and you have just received an email from one of them who indicates that she wants to exchange her park for a larger one. She has asked for an appointment with you when she is in town next week to talk about and probably list the property with you. Describe how you would prepare for this meeting.

2. You are at a mobile home park that is your listing to meet another broker who wants to show it. Once there, she aggressively insists on your letting her and her client see 10 of the park-owned homes, although this was not requested previously. What would you do, and why?

3. You are at a listing appointment with an elderly lady who owns a mobile home park. She has asked you to list the property and tells you that every dollar she can get is precious to her at her age. She does not know that a neighborhood retail shopping center with a chain grocery store as the anchor tenant is scheduled for construction in six months. You know about it because you keep up on the commercial marketplace. What would you do, and why?

4. You have been saving 20% of your commission checks for some time, and you now have enough saved to invest in a mobile home park, which you specialize in. The owner of a well-located but totally non-amenity park with lots of open space on the 7 acres he owns calls you and asks you to list the property. What steps would you take with the owner, and what do you see as a possible way to greatly increase the value and rents of the park?

5. You are with the managing partner of a limited liability company who has asked you to list the $2.5-million mobile home park the company owns. Describe what documents and information you will need from her, and why they are important.

Chapter 26

Industrial Properties

284   *Chapter 26*

Industrial property is in a class by itself. It comes in all shapes and sizes, from light industrial warehouse, showroom, and office space to heavy industrial properties such as cement factories, heavy equipment repair facilities, and automobile-manufacturing plants.

This is an area you should not venture into by yourself until you are highly educated about the problems that can be encountered with industrial property. It takes at least two or three years to reach an acceptable level of competency.

"What's the big deal," you say to yourself. Industrial property is primarily used for the manufacture, storage, sale, and/or transfer of goods, although automobile showrooms and repair facilities, self-storage facilities, and light industrial space that is leased for restaurant facilities are also classified as special-purpose industrial property. It is highly regulated as to zoning issues, environmental issues, height limitations, easements, and public resistance to its uses and proximity to residential neighborhoods.

Light Industrial Space

Light industrial space can be wood-frame/stucco finish, which is mostly found in older industrial property, but for many years now concrete tilt-up buildings are the norm. The concrete walls are poured flat, and once sufficiently hardened they are tilted into place. Then, the roof trusses and ceiling are installed, the insulation is put in place, and the roofing material is installed. These light industrial properties are most often found in industrial parks today, where many buildings are constructed at the same time and the area marketed as a new industrial park. Nearly all those are subject to covenants, conditions, and restrictions, much like a residential subdivision. When you are representing a buyer or prospective tenant in these types of properties, it is proper client representation to ask the clients to get their company's financial statement together because the owners of the property they select will certainly ask for it. You should remember to keep this statement confidential.

Heavy Industrial Space

Heavy industrial property brings its own set of issues you may need to deal with. Electrical loads are of paramount importance, and you will often be asked what the electrical load is (it can run from standard 140 amps to 440 amps/three-phase electrical power or more), as well as whether the prospective purchaser or lessee needs access to a railroad spur to bring rail cars into their plant to off-load or on-load. Ceiling height, as well as the number of support posts that are in the space, can be quite important to purchasers and lessees of either type of industrial space. Modern buildings are built using flying buttresses, often called "glue-lams," which means there are virtually no support posts holding up the roof, as is found in older properties. This modern style of construction allows the new owners or lessees much more flexibility in their space planning than do older properties. There is diminished value in the older properties because of this fact. Space planning will very often require the prospective purchaser or lessee to ask the sellers for tenant improvements (TIs). Many owners will negotiate to amortize the cost of any TIs provided over the term of the initial lease period; other owners will offer a fixed dollar amount per square foot of space purchased or leased. These are expensive, so be careful, and get advice from the old-timers when you are involved in TI negotiations. Tenant improvements often entail the remodel or installation of restrooms. If you encounter this, be sure that the plans and installation meet current ADA standards. Your local city building department will give you a copy of the requirements, or you can download them from the Internet.

286   *Chapter 26*

Pollution

One of the worst and costliest lawsuits you could ever be involved in is when you represent a client who purchases or sells an industrial property with nondisclosed or improperly disclosed hydrocarbon or other pollution on the property; this is especially problematic if the pollution has penetrated the groundwater. Settlements of these types of problems can run in the millions of dollars.

I want to give you an example of a proper way to cover yourself and the clients you represent. I sold a small, closed-down industrial property on the San Francisco Peninsula. They used to make resins there; there was noted pollution when the plant was shut down, and there were five closed test wells on the property. I drove the client to the Environmental Protection Agency (EPA) office in Oakland, and we obtained the full set of paperwork that dealt with the problem and the closure, including the San Mateo County Final Clearance. The pollution had been dug up and disposed of (a very costly issue) several years before. Because most of the premises was covered with cement for parking, during our 120-day escrow period I advised my client by telephone, as well as several times in writing, to have the cement broken open in several areas to check for additional pollution. He elected not to. The escrow closed, and shortly after, the EPA required him to break up some cement near the closed test holes that surrounded the old pollution site. On doing so, the workers found additional pollution. Approximately 10 days later I received a call from his attorney asking for my escrow file. Luckily, I have always kept excellent notes, including printing out and saving sent emails, which were also in my file. The attorney called me a month or so later and said, "Well, you're squeaky clean, but the county sure has a problem!" It turns out that there was to be a three-phase closure of the property, but only two phases were completed. The county had signed off on the property, certifying it to be free of any further pollution, without ever conducting Phase 3, which was to check under the cement. The attorney told me that I may be called as a witness, but I never heard from any of them again.

If you are representing a buyer or lessee, be sure to ask what your client's needs are and investigate thoroughly. These light industrial buildings are often leased or purchased by retail clients who need a high traffic count and therefore good street visibility for their exterior sign, and so these are questions you will need to ask them and concerns to address. If the client is leasing, you need to ask how long of a lease he/she wants. It is common for prospective tenants to want only a three-year lease to limit their financial exposure in the event their business fails, maybe with a three- to five-year right to renew. Explain to them that if they are comfortable with the future success of the business they are opening, the longer the lease term they ask for, the better they are able to negotiate with the owners about the rent and TIs. Always ask your buyer or lessee clients if they have any special electric power needs. Many types of manufacturing require a very high amperage, and you need to investigate this as part of your obligation of due diligence, especially with any property they have identified as a potential acquisition.

Heavy industrial properties are often purchased or leased by firms that require "dock-high" loading ramps. Dock-highs are overhead doors that raise and open at a height that is nearly or exactly equal in height to the rear of a semi-truck's trailer; they allow workers to drive a forklift into the rear of the semi's trailer to off-load or on-load heavy materials. If your client states that he/she needs a heavy industrial space, question the client thoroughly to ascertain all his/her needs, and if dock-highs are required, ask how many at a minimum or maximum. Ask about electrical load requirements, ceiling heights, railway spurs, and any signage visibility needs. I always ask clients to describe their "perfect property" to me. I take many notes, being sure we have covered the requirements listed here.

288   *Chapter 26*

One last time, I caution you to go slow when entering this specialty and urge you to train thoroughly while shadowing a mentor or experienced agent to the extent possible. If you work with one of these seasoned professionals, you will, for a time, perhaps as much as a year or longer, probably share with your mentor a portion of any commissions you generate. Keep in mind that this is the best money you will ever have spent on your professional education!

Review Questions

1. Which of the following should you ask or request of your new client before showing her industrial property?
   A. request a copy of her and her company's current financial statement
   B. ask her to describe her perfect property
   C. find out if she require high ceilings and/or a railroad spur
   D. all of the answer choices

2. Which of the following statements is true?
   A. The public shows little interest in regulating the location of industrial property.
   B. Industrial property is highly regulated by zoning restrictions.
   C. The Americans with Disabilities Act does not apply to light industrial properties.
   D. Height limitations are not regulated for heavy industrial properties.

3. Which statement is true of new industrial parks?
   A. More-than-adequate parking is available.
   B. Manufacturing facilities are not allowed.
   C. They are built only for heavy industrial properties.
   D. They nearly always have recorded covenants, conditions, and restrictions.

4. Which of the following signal(s) possible or probable hydro-carbon pollution?
   A. large, dark stains on the ground
   B. in-ground test wells in a large circle
   C. a smell of oil or gas as you walk through the closed interior of a building
   D. all of the answer choices

5. Which of the following would NOT be classified as an industrial property?
   A. cement manufacturing plant
   B. copper mine cargo truck repair facility
   C. neighborhood center with a gas station on the premises
   D. auto repair shop

Class Discussion Topics

1. Discuss how to elicit a client's needs prior to showing him/her property.
2. Name as many types of heavy industrial real estate as you can, and tell us what are important issues to investigate with each one.
3. What important role do covenants, conditions, and restrictions play in an industrial warehouse business park? What could happen if they were not in place or enforced?
4. Why do hydrocarbon spills create such a major problem in industrial properties? What must you, as the real estate professional, do to see that your client is protected?
5. Your client owns a highly successful copy machine sales and servicing business. His space is too small for his expanding organization, and he has asked you to find him a 10,000-square-foot space to move his business into. He relies heavily on drive-by traffic. What are important issues you will need to consider when showing him space?

Appendix 1: Sample Annual Property Operating Data (APOD)

Property Name	Windwood Apartments		Purchase Price	1,622,183		
Location	1010 N Craycroft Blvd		Plus Acquisition costs	27,577	1.7% est	
Property Type	Multi-family		Less New Loans	1,216,637	75%	
# units/SF	52		Equals total Investment	433,120		
				Annual	Int	
			Loan Balance	payment	Rate	Term
			1st 1,216,637	73,974	4.50%	30 yrs
			2nd			
Annual figures			Comments			
	INCOME	EXPENSES				
Scheduled rent	291,840					
Vac/concessions		26,265	17,510 / 8,755			
Effective rent	265,575					
Other income	13,740					
Operating Income	279,314					
Administration						
RE Taxes		20,151				
Insurance		11,172				
Off-site Mgt		0	See accn't/legal			
On-site Mgr		11,173				
Repairs/maint		36,000				
Water		45,000	Incl: gas, electric, cable			
Gas						
Electricity						
Cable						
Accnt'g/Legal		5,200				
Licenses/permits						
Advertising		2,600				
Supplies			Incl. in maint/repairs			
Contract Svcs						
Total Expenses		146,292	52.38%			
Net Op Income	133,019					
Debt Service		73,974				
Leasing Fees						
Reserves						
Cash Flow		59,045				
Cap Rate		8.2				
Cash-on-Cash return with loan reduction			59,045 + 19,627 = 78,672 / 433,120 = 18.6%			
Cash-on-Cash return without loan reduction			59,045 / 433,120 = 13.63%			

The figures contained herein are deemed to be reliable; however, the client is cautioned to make his or her separate investigation during the escrow Due Diligence period.

Appendix 2: Sample Letter of Intent (LOI)

SKYLINE DEVELOPMENT CO., LLC
11165 N. La Canada Drive, Suite 175, Oro Valley,
Arizona 85737
Office: 520.555.2403
Fax: 520.555.8837

December 11, 2017
Mr. Barry Edwards,
Tucson, Arizona

RE: Sale of approximately [H11006]147.32 acres of vacant land, Pima County Assessor's #831-92-300B, 8160,8260,8360 (the "**Property**")

Dear Mr. Edwards:

The purpose of this letter is to indicate the basis upon which Mr. Barry Edwards (the "**Seller**") is prepared to proceed with the sale of the Property, subject to the completion and execution of a definitive written purchase and sale agreement satisfactory to both parties and their respective counsel.

PROPERTY:	Vacant land containing approximately 147.32 acres in Tucson, Arizona, and controlled by Pima County
PURCHASER:	Skyline Development Co., LLC, an Arizona limited liability company (the "**Purchaser**")
PURCHASE PRICE:	Two Million Eight Hundred Thousand Dollars and no Cents ($2,800,000.00); or Three Million Three Hundred Fifty Two Thousand Dollars and no Cents ($3,352,000) if seller agrees to a Fifty % carryback at 7.5% for a period not to exceed Fourteen Months. Seller shall be paid interest payments quarterly and purchaser reserves the right to prepay the entire principal balance at any time without penalty.
EARNEST MONEY:	Purchaser shall deposit Thirty Five Thousand Dollars ($35,000.00) into escrow with the escrow agent defined below within 48 hours after the execution of the Purchase Agreement. Upon expiration of the due diligence period, Purchaser shall deposit an additional Sixty-Five Thousand Dollars ($65,000.00) for a total of One Hundred Thousand Dollars and no Cents ($100,000.00). Earnest money shall be deposited with Title Security Agency, Inc., 6970 N. Oracle Road, Suite 201, Tucson, Arizona 85704, (520) 555-1212, and to the attention of Mrs. Elaine Johnson (the "Escrow Agent").

Sample Letter of Intent (LOI)   295

	Earnest money shall become non-refundable at the end of the due diligence period, unless the purchase and sale contract is appropriately terminated by Purchaser. All monies shall be used as part of the down payment and/or appropriate closing costs.
DUE DILIGENCE PERIOD:	Sixty days (60) days from full execution of the Purchase Agreement by both parties.
DUE DILIGENCE REPORTS:	All due diligence studies and reports shall be the responsibility of Purchaser and at Purchaser's expense. All administration concerning the Property, not limited to and to include Alta survey, topographical within a 2 ft contour, engineering and hydrological data, site assessment and biological impact data shall be released in digital format from Seller or Seller's agents to Purchaser or to Purchaser's agents and are to be made immediately upon mutual Purchase Agreement execution and available to Seller.
PURCHASER'S INVESTIGATION RIGHTS:	The Property is being sold "AS IS" without warranty or representation as to its physical condition, compliance with current codes or fitness for a particular purpose. At Purchaser's sole discretion, Purchaser or its authorized representatives shall be entitled to enter upon the Property and make such surveying, engineering, physical, and other studies as Purchaser deems fit.

	Prior to any such entry upon the Property, Purchaser shall sign a right of entry and nondisclosure agreement, provide notice to Seller of its intended scope of work and Purchaser shall indemnify Seller as to its actions and its authorized representative's and contractor's actions on the Property, during the performance of the investigation.
	Purchaser may perform an environmental Phase I study on the Property. However, should a Phase II be desired, Purchaser must obtain Seller's agreement on the scope of the work and obtain Seller's written approval.
	After all such investigation, if Purchaser in its sole discretion determines that the Property is not satisfactory to Purchaser, then Purchaser may terminate the transaction by notifying Seller in writing no later than the end of the due diligence period.
TITLE & SURVEY:	Seller shall convey its fee simple interest in the Property by a special warranty deed subject to items of record.
CLOSING:	Property will be placed in escrow upon full execution of the purchase and sale agreement and closing will occur at the expiration of Forty-Five (45) days from date of the successful completion of the due diligence period.

Sample Letter of Intent (LOI) **297**

CLOSING COSTS:	Seller shall pay for the owner's title insurance policy, extended coverage, and all endorsements. Purchaser shall pay for the cost of any survey, if necessary. Purchaser shall pay for the costs incurred in connection with its physical inspection of the Property. Other normal costs associated with the closing, including recording fees, escrow fees, and transfer taxes, shall be paid and split according to local custom and practice in the local market. The purchase price shall be adjusted in accordance with generally accepted accounting principles for real estate taxes, credits, and other adjustments.
BROKERAGE COMMISSION:	The parties represent and warrant that Herd Realty Corporation and Sunshine Realty Company, Inc., will be paid a 6% commission, 3% each to the listing and sales office for a real estate broker's commission.
CONTRACT:	Upon execution of this letter by both parties, Purchaser will draft the proposed purchase and sale agreement, which shall be submitted to Seller for review and comment. Both parties agree to employ the appropriate resources to use reasonable efforts to execute a purchase and sale agreement within Fifteen (15) business days after Seller's receipt of this LOI.

298   *Appendix 2*

BACKUP BUYER:	Purchaser acknowledges that prior to closing, Seller may negotiate a sale of the Property to another entity (the "Backup Buyer"), pursuant to a contract, letter of understanding, other writing, or oral agreement. The rights of the Backup Buyer with respect to the Property will expire upon the closing herein. If Purchaser and Seller negotiate, execute, and deliver a purchase and sale contract with respect to the Property that is subsequently terminated, then Seller may sell the Property to the Backup Buyer or any other buyer at any time free and clear of any claim of Purchaser. Purchaser will render reasonable cooperation prior to closing hereunder to permit the Backup Buyer to concurrently perform its due diligence investigation at no cost to Purchaser and so long as the Backup Buyer does not interfere with Purchaser's due diligence investigation.
CONFIDENTIALITY:	Seller and Purchaser shall keep all information and reports obtained from Seller relating to the Property or the proposed transaction confidential and will not disclose any such confidential information to any other person or entity without obtaining the prior written consent of Seller and Purchaser. If a purchase and sale agreement is executed by the parties, Purchaser and

Sample Letter of Intent (LOI) **299**

	Seller shall keep all terms of the purchase and sale agreement confidential and may disclose only such terms as are necessary to each party's attorneys, accountants, and other professional advisors.
ANNOUNCEMENTS:	Seller and Purchaser shall consult with each other in advance with regard to all press releases and other announcements issued concerning this transaction or the transactions contemplated hereby and, except as may be required by applicable laws or the applicable rules and regulations of any governmental agency, neither Seller nor Purchaser shall issue any press release, Internet article or other such publicity without the prior written consent of the other party, which consent may be granted or withheld in the consenting party's sole discretion.
REMEDIES:	The terms of the Purchase and Sale Agreement and escrow instructions shall govern remedies in the event either party terminates the purchase and sale contract or cancels escrow.
APPROVAL:	This transaction is expressly contingent upon obtaining a review and approval from Purchaser's legal counsel regarding the subsequent executed Purchase Agreement and written approval thereof during the due diligence period.

300   *Appendix 2*

NONBINDING AGREEMENT:	Other than the confidentiality provisions of Section 14 herein, this letter is a **nonbinding** proposal and no party shall have the right to institute any legal actions with respect to the transaction described herein.

Seller and Purchaser acknowledge that this nonbinding proposal is not an offer, and that it is intended only as the basis for setting forth general terms and conditions and for further negotiation for the Property described herein. Either party can terminate negotiations at any time without any liability to the other party and neither party shall have any obligation to negotiate in good faith. The parties acknowledge that the terms contained herein do not include all of the material terms and conditions which would be required in a definitive agreement. Both parties agree that only a final agreement containing all of the terms required by both Purchaser and Seller, executed by each party and placed in escrow, will constitute a binding agreement for a purchase of the Property, subject to the rights of other parties. Seller has until 5:00 P.M., Mountain Standard Time, on November 30, 2017, to provide a written response to this Letter of Intent.

AGREED AND ACCEPTED AND ACKNOWLEDGED THIS _____ DAY OF November, 2017:

SELLER: PURCHASER:
                                By: Skyline Development Co., LLC

_____   _____

By: Mr. Barry Edwards   By: William Claussen, Managing
                                Partner

_____   _____

By: By:

About the Author

Bob Herd started his real estate career in early 1972 with a small real estate company on the San Francisco Peninsula.

Although no formal training programs or systems were available in those days, Bob used some good initial training from his branch manager, his natural ability to interact with people, and his keen intuition about human nature to sell more than 60 homes in his first and second years in the business. He was awarded the coveted "Top Salesperson" award from the real estate association that he belonged to in 1974.

Bob's wife, Eileen, was licensed in 1975 and became his licensed assistant on a part-time basis until their four children were grown; she then became his full-time assistant. Her help was very instrumental in his receipt of the "Top Salesperson" award and his continuing success throughout his career in sales.

Although Bob opened his own highly successful company in 1974, he still remained very active in commercial real estate sales, and under his training and guidance, one of his agents won the "Top Salesperson" award from the same association every year for the next six years, except for 1979.

Over the course of his career, which spans more than 46 years, Bob has been a salesperson, broker/owner, branch manager, and regional manager for some of the largest real estate companies in the San Francisco Bay Area and Tucson, Arizona. Whether he was in a sales position or a nonselling management position, he always maintained and nurtured in his associates a keen sense of the ever-evolving sensible, human-nature-based style of professionally handling the needs of customers and clients and the far-reaching effectiveness of working with a top licensed assistant.

Bob maintains both a California and an Arizona broker's license and holds the Certified Residential Brokerage Manager (CRB), Certified Residential Specialist (CRS), and Graduate, Realtors Institute (GRI) designations. He is currently a commercial broker with Keller Williams Commercial Division in Tucson, Arizona. You may reach Bob at (520) 481-2888 or by email at bherd1945@gmail.com. He is happy to help you with any questions you may have.

Chapter Review Questions Answer Key

Chapter 1

1. D
2. D
3. A
4. C
5. D

Chapter 2

1. D
2. C
3. A
4. D
5. D

Chapter 3

1. D
2. C
3. A
4. A
5. A

Chapter 4

1. B
2. D
3. D
4. B
5. A

Chapter 5

1. C
2. D
3. D
4. A
5. A

Chapter 6

1. A
2. C
3. D
4. A
5. C

Chapter 7

1. A
2. D
3. C
4. A
5. C

Chapter 8

1. D
2. D
3. C
4. B
5. A

Chapter 9

1. D
2. A
3. A
4. A
5. A

Chapter 10

1. B
2. D
3. A
4. D
5. D

Chapter Review Questions Answer Key 305

Chapter 11

1. D
2. A
3. A
4. D
5. C

Chapter 12

1. A
2. D
3. A
4. B
5. D

Chapter 13

1. B
2. C
3. D
4. D
5. C

Chapter 14

1. D
2. D
3. D
4. A
5. A

Chapter 15

1. D
2. A
3. A
4. B
5. B

Chapter 16

1. C
2. C
3. D
4. D
5. C

306 *Chapter Review Questions Answer Key*

Chapter 17

1. A
2. C
3. C
4. D
5. A

Chapter 18

1. D
2. C
3. A
4. B
5. D

Chapter 19

1. A
2. B
3. D
4. D
5. D

Chapter 20

1. C
2. B
3. C
4. D
5. C

Chapter 21

1. D
2. B
3. B
4. A
5. C

Chapter 22

1. B
2. D
3. A
4. D
5. D

Chapter Review Questions Answer Key 307

Chapter 23

1. A
2. B
3. B
4. D
5. C

Chapter 24

1. D
2. D
3. A
4. C
5. A

Chapter 25

1. C
2. A
3. C
4. D
5. A

Chapter 26

1. D
2. B
3. B
4. A
5. C

Index

accelerated cost recovery
system (ACRS), 73
accordion income, 44
accounting records, in property
management, 155–156
Accredited Management
Organization (AMO),
150–151
ACRS (accelerated cost
recovery system), 73
ADA. *See* Americans with
Disabilities Act
adjusted basis, 76
ADS (annual debt service), 143
advertising
AIDA formula, 113
in listing proposals, 106
in newspapers, 112
size of, 114
style of, 114
advice for success
Bruce Suppes, 176–177
Debbie Green, 182
Gary Best, 179–180
Harvey Mordka, 178–179
Maureen Vosburgh, 181
Pete Peterson, 177–178
after-tax cash flow, 72
AIDA formula, 113
amenities, 221

of mobile home parks, 276,
277
Americans with Disabilities Act
(ADA), 150, 285
violation of, 165
AMO (Accredited Management
Organization), 150–151
amortization periods, 145
anchor tenant, 241
annual business plan
month 1, 84–86
month 2, 86–88
month 3, 88–89
month 4, 89–90
month 5, 90
month 6, 91
month 7, 91–92
month 8, 92–93
month 9, 93–94
month 10, 94–95
month 11, 95–96
month 12, 96–97
monthly mailings in, 84
year-end assessment, 97
annual debt service (ADS), 143
annual maintenance fees, 221
Annual Property Operating
Data (APOD), 69, 291
purchase agreement and,
126

310 *Index*

annual rent escalation clause, 172–173
annual straight-line depreciation allowance, 75
antidiscrimination, 164–165
Apache Junction, 19, 108
APOD. *See* Annual Property Operating Data
applied knowledge, 28
Arizona, 16–17, 108, 165, 270
assets, selling, 10
assignment, in property management, 158–159
assistants
  hiring, 44–45
  licensed, 45–46
authorized signatory, 7

Banana Republic, 242
Bay Area, 104
Become a Mega-Producer Real Estate Agent: Profit from a Licensed Assistant (Herd), 45
Best, Gary, 179–180
Biggs decision, 79
binders, 37, 105
body language, 108
boots, 79
borrowing, 10
branding, 112
brokerage commission, 297
brownfields, 270
bulk mail, 84
Burger King, 241–242, 256
Business and Professions Code, 156

business politeness, 107
buyer's representative, 134–138

California, 221
capitalization of net income method. *See* cap rate
cap rate, 29, 65, 115
  multifamily complexes and, 222
  for property valuation, 67–71
cash flow, 9
  after-tax, 72
  pretax, 72
  before taxes, 70
cash-on-cash method, for property valuation, 70–71
cash reserves, 231
CBRE Commercial Brokerage, 186–190
CB Richard Ellis, 5
CCIM. *See* Certified Commercial Investment Member
CC&Rs (covenants, conditions, and restrictions), 232
certificates of deposit (CDs), 258
Certified Commercial Investment Member (CCIM), 5, 8, 49, 147, 199
  chapter meetings, 88–93, 97
  courses leading to, 25
  marketing and, 116
  qualification for, 73
  value of, 28
Certified Property Manager (CPM), 150–151
Certified Residential Brokerage Manager (CRB), 49

Index 311

Chapman/Lindsey, 198–199
cleaning, in commercial leases, 168
client representation, in commercial lease, 169–171
closing attorneys, 27
closing costs, nonrecurring, 75
Code of Ethics, 57
cold-calling
  commercial business owners, 55
  follow-ups, 56
  homeowners, 54
  introductions in, 55–56
  property owners, 54, 56–57
  as prospecting, 54
Coldwell Banker Commercial, 5, 8, 198–199
commercial business owners, cold-calling, 55
commercial leases
  antidiscrimination in, 164–165
  cleaning in, 168
  client representation in, 169–171
  copies of, 135, 136
  dates in, 166
  description of premises in, 166
  exculpatory clause in, 168
  late charges in, 167
  names of parties in, 166
  pets in, 167
  premises inspection, 167
  provisions, 165–166

  rent schedules in, 167
  right of entry in, 168–169
  security deposits in, 168
  termination of, 159
  waterbeds in, 167
commercial real estate, 4
  advantages of, 6–7
  entry into, 6
  seminars, 90
commission checks, 5
  amounts, 104
commissionectomy, 125
Commissioner's Preliminary Subdivision Public Report, 265–266
comparable sales book, 86
comp books, 36, 90, 108
  building, 37
  credibility and, 37–38
  listing proposals and, 106
  updating, 95
concrete block construction, 249
confidentiality, 298
constructive receipt, 78
Consumer Price Index (CPI), 173, 231, 256
contact persons, 94
contamination, 270
CoStar, 7, 84–86, 223
  emergence of, 8
  LoopNet and, 115
  subscription to, 64
Costco, 241, 242
counteroffers, 126
covenants, conditions, and restrictions (CC&Rs), 232

312 *Index*

CPI (Consumer Price Index),
 173, 231, 256
CPM (Certified Property
 Manager), 150–151
CRB (Certified Residential
 Brokerage Manager), 49
credibility, 30, 103
 comp books and, 37–38
 respect and, 36–37
credit losses, 69–70
credit unions, 146
crime rates, 257
cross-easements, 239

databases, 57
 current, 94
 double-checking, 91
D'Avanzo, Andrew, 74
*D'Avanzo v. United States of
 America*, 74
DBA (doing business as), 229
debt coverage ratio, 143
 examples of, 144
debt services, 69, 70
deductions, 73
 depreciation allowance and, 74
 land and, 74
Department of Real Estate, 268
depreciation allowance
 annual straight-line, 75
 computation of, 75–76
 deductions and, 74
 federal tax table for, 76
 general depreciation
  system method, 76
 taxation and, 73

depreciation recapture, 77
description of premises, in
 commercial leases, 166
digital tape recorder, 133
Dillard's, 164
direct deeding, 78
dock-high loading ramps, 286
doing business as (DBA), 229
Do Not Call list, 54
double-wide units, 276–277
drop-dead clause, in
 purchase agreement, 122
due diligence period,
 136–137, 267, 270, 295

earnest money, 294
earthquake zones, 270
education, role-playing and, 25–26
ego, 46
emancipated minors, 166
emotional fulfillment, 18
Environmental Protection
 Agency (EPA), 25, 286
Environmental Site Assessment
 Phase 1, 24, 240
 Phase 2, 240
 Phase 3, 24–25, 240
EPA (Environmental Protection
 Agency), 25, 286
escrow, 27
 agents, 135
 closing, 78, 121, 137
 communications during,
  133–134
 conduction of, 123
 exchange, 79

Index 313

listing agent in, 130–134
opening, 79, 130
in purchase agreement, 123
timeline, 131
in United States, 130
Estoppel Certificates, 121, 131
signing, 135
evictions, 159
retaliatory, 160
exchange escrow, 79
exclusive agency listing, 102–103
exclusive authorization and
right to sell, 102
exculpatory clause, in
commercial lease, 168
expansion, office buildings
and, 228
experience, 7

fast food, 241–242
faxes, 134
federal tax table for, depreciation allowance, 76
Final Subdivision Public Report,
266
floating foundations, 249
flood zones, 270
follow-up calls, 87, 89
Fortune 500, 256
full-service lease, 171–172
future value estimation, 143

general depreciation system
method, 76
GOI (gross operating income),
64, 68, 70

Goldberg, Mark, 115
Green, Debbie, 182
GRM. *See* gross rent multiplier
gross lease, 171
modified, 172, 230
for office buildings, 230
gross operating income (GOI),
64, 68, 70
gross rent multiplier (GRM), 65
for property valuation, 66–67
utilization of, 66–67
gross scheduled income
(GSI), 68
rental, 69–70
GroupMe, 195
GSI. *See* gross scheduled income

hand-delivery, 134
Happy Holiday cards, 96
heavy industrial space, 285
hidden assets, 6
Home Depot, 242
home equity, 10
*How to Become a Mega-Producer
Real Estate Agent in Five Years*
(Herd), 54
hydrocarbon businesses, 240

improvements, 74–75
income, rate of return, value
(IRV), 67–68
income streams, 143
individual property manager,
151
industrial properties, 146–147
heavy, 285

314   *Index*

light, 284–285
pollution and, 286–288
inside sales associate (ISA), 46
    hiring, 48
Institute of Real Estate
    Management (IREM),
    150–151
intent clause, in purchase
    agreement, 124
intermediaries, IRS on, 78
internal rate of return (IRR), 65
    calculation of, 72
    for property valuation, 72–77
Internal Revenue Service (IRS)
    Code Section 1031, 79,
        202–203
    on intermediaries, 78
    on tax-deferred exchanges,
        79
Internet, 114–115
interviews, 54
introductory letters, 85,
    87, 89
investigation rights, 295
investment properties, driving
    by, 56
investors, cold-calling and, 55
iPads, 37
IREM (Institute of Real Estate
    Management), 150–151
IRR. *See* internal rate of return
IRS. *See* Internal Revenue
    Service
IRV (income, rate or return,
    value), 67–68
ISA. *See* inside sales associate

J.C. Penny, 164, 242
Jiffy Lube, 256
jpegs, 37

Keller Williams, 193
K-Mart, 256

land
    deductions and, 74
    raw, 269–271
land brokerage
    of divided lots in existing
        subdivisions, 264–265
    of large estate-type
        acreage, 268–269
    of newly subdivided land,
        266–267
    of raw land, 269–271
landlord's responsibilities,
    in property management,
    157–158
laptops, 37
large estate-type acreage, land
    brokerage of, 268–269
late charges, in commercial
    leases, 167
leases. *See specific types*
legal counsel, 122
lessee, 164
lessor, 164
letter of intent (LOI), 170
    in purchase agreement,
        124–125
    redlining, 171
    sample, 293–300
licensed assistants, 45–46

Index 315

licensed property manager, 151
light industrial space, 284–285
limited liability companies
 (LLCs), 7, 64, 85, 131
 agreements with, 122–123
Lindsey, Paul, 8, 198–205
listing agent, in escrow,
 130–134
listing appointment,
 role-playing, 26
listing proposal book, 87, 89
 setups and, 88
 trust and, 107
listing proposals
 advertising plan in, 106
 comp books and, 106
 creating, 105–106
 exclusive agency,
 102–103
 exclusive authorization and
 right to sell, 102
 open, 102
 sections, 105–106
 types of, 102
 verbal, 103–104
listings, obtaining, 38
LLCs. *See* limited liability
 companies
loan information, 133, 136
loan-to-value ratio (LTV), 143,
 239
LOI. *See* letter of intent
LoopNet, 84–86, 223
 CoStar and, 115
 subscription to, 64
LTV. *See* loan-to-value ratio

Macy's, 242
MAI (Member of the Appraiser's
 Institute), 72
Marcus & Millichap Commercial
 Brokerage, 5
market data method, for
 property valuation, 71–72
marketing, 115
 CCIM and, 116
maximum loan amount, 144–147
MBA, 28
McDonald's, 241–242, 256
Member of the Appraiser's
 Institute (MAI), 72
mentors, 24
Mercantile Trust decision, 79
metal buildings, 249
MID-AMERICA Real Estate
 Corporation, 115
Midas Muffler, 256
MLS. *See* multiple listing service
mobile home parks
 amenities of, 276, 277
 common-area issues, 278–280
 double-wide units, 276–277
 location, 277
 park-owned units, 278
 resident manager of, 279
 single-wide units, 276–277
modified gross lease, 172
 for office buildings, 230
monthly expenses, 9
monthly mailings, in annual
 business plan, 84
Mordka, Harvey, 178–179
mortgage underwriting, 142

316 *Index*

multifamily complexes, 220
  brokerage, 222
  cap rate and, 222
  maintenance of, 221
  rehabilitation of, 223–224
multiple listing service (MLS), 8
  access to, 58
  National Association of
    REALTORS® and, 58
  in United States, 116
mutual maintenance agreement,
  220–221
mutual referral agreement, 58

National Association of
  REALTORS®, 5, 25, 49, 73
  Code of Ethics, 57
  MLS and, 58
National Realty Trust (NRT),
  199
nest eggs, 8–9
net-net-net (NNN) lease, 18, 172
  for office buildings, 230
  reviewing, 257
  taxes and, 256–257
net operating income (NOI), 64,
  68–70, 143
newly licensed real estate agents,
  4–5
newly subdivided land, land
  brokerage of, 266–267
newsletters, 94
newspapers, advertising in, 112
NNN least. *See* net-net-net lease
NOI (net operating income), 64,
  68–70, 143

nonbinding agreement, 300
nonrecurring closing costs, 75
NRT (National Realty Trust), 199

office buildings
  age of, 231
  economic downturns and, 231
  expansion and, 228
  financing, 228
  gross lease for, 230
  locations of, 230
  modified gross lease for, 230
  square footage, 229
open listing, 103
operating expenses, 70
outside sales associate (OSA), 46
  hiring, 48
owner-occupied buildings, 220

parking
  resurfacing, 240
  at retail centers, 238–239
perfect property, 286
performance standards, 17–18
pest inspection, 136–137
Petco, 164
Peterson, Pete, 44, 190–197
  advice for success, 177–178
pets, in commercial leases, 167
Phoenix, 36
planned unit developments
  (PUDs), 212
pocket listing. *See* verbal listing
pollution, 146
  industrial properties and,
    286–288

PowerPoint, 105
preliminary title report, 132
premises inspection, in
    commercial leases, 167
presentation, 107–109
pretax cash flow, 72
pride, 18
properties, run-down, 38
property management, 96
    accounting records, 155–156
    assignment in, 158–159
    firms, 151
    individual property
        manager, 151
    landlord's responsibilities in,
        157–158
    licensed property manager,
        151
    rent schedules in, 154–155
    resident manager, 151
    specialization in, 150
    specific duties, 153–154
    state-defined responsibilities
        in, 152–153
    sublease in, 158–159
    tenant's responsibilities in,
        156–157
property owners
    cold-calling, 54, 56–57
    prospecting and, 56–57
property valuation, 29
    cap rate for, 67–71
    cash-on-cash method for,
        70–71
    GRM for, 66–67
    IRR for, 72–77

market data method for,
    71–72
methods, 64
prospecting
    cold-calling as, 54
    daily commitments to, 86
    property owners and, 56–57
    referral systems and, 57–59
PUDs (planned unit
    developments), 212
purchase agreement, 131–132,
    136, 294
    APOD and, 126
    commercial, 120–121
    defining, 27
    drop-dead clause in, 122
    escrow in, 123
    intent clause in, 124
    letter of intent in, 124–125
    role-playing, 26–30
    signing, 125–126

rate of return, 68
raw land, land brokerage of,
    269–271
Reagan administration, 73
Real Data, 73
real estate agents
    newly licensed, 4–5
    residential, 4–5
real estate investment trusts
    (REITs), 18–19, 72, 74, 108
    agreements with, 122–123
Real Estate Settlement
    Procedures Act (RESPA), 223
REALTOR® magazine, 55–56

318   *Index*

REALTORS® Land Institute
(RLI), 271
recapture, depreciation, 77
referral systems, 8
  mutual referral agreement,
  58
  prospecting and, 57–59
regional malls, 242
rehabilitation, of multifamily
  complexes, 223–224
REITs. *See* real estate investment
  trusts
rental survey, 64
  conducting, 88
  quarterly, 91, 94
  reception of, 89
rent control, 214
rent schedules
  in commercial leases, 167
  in property management,
  154–155
repairs, 133
replacement properties, 78–79
residential real estate agents,
  4–5
  lists of top, 57–58
  time blocking for, 6
resident manager, 151
  of mobile home parks, 279
  requirements of, 221
  of self-storage facilities, 250
RESPA (Real Estate Settlement
  Procedures Act), 223
respect, credibility and, 36–37
retail centers, 36
  neighborhood, 241

parking at, 238–239
size of, 238
retaliatory evictions, 160
retirement plans, 9
right of entry, in commercial
  lease, 168–169
rights of rescission time
  limits, 266
risk aversion, 142
risk/reward factor, 222
risks, 24
RLI (REALTORS® Land
  Institute), 271
Robinsons-May, 242
Rogers, Clyde, 16
role-playing
  education and, 25–26
  listing appointment, 26
  purchase agreement
  presentation, 27–30
  purchase agreement
  writing, 26–27
roof inspection, 136–137
run-down properties, 38

Safeway, 241, 256
Salvation Army, 19
San Francisco, 35, 121–122, 228
San Francisco Examiner, 113
San Mateo County Financial
  Clearance, 288
savings, 9
Schedule C, 120, 131
Sears, 164, 242
self-discipline, 17
self-storage facilities

Index 319

construction of, 248
operating expenses, 248
resident manager of, 250
site location of, 251
seller's representative, in escrow, 130–134
selling agents, 134–138
selling assets, 10
setups, 24
listing proposal book and, 88
70-hour syndrome, 48
simultaneous closings, 78
single-family homes and condominiums
advantages, 211–212
disadvantages, 213–217
single-wide units, 276–277
slurry coat, 239
sparkling, 30
specialization, need for, 34
spousal support, 6
Starker decision, 79
Starker delayed exchange, 77–78
state-defined responsibilities, in property management, 152–153
Stockman, David, 73
Stratton Group, 192
strip centers, 238
Subchapter S corporations, 229
subdivided lots in existing subdivisions, land brokerage of, 264–265
sublease, in property management, 158–159
success. *See* advice for success

Suppes, Bruce, 165, 186–190
advice for success, 176–177

Target, 164, 242, 256
tax-deferred exchanges, 77–78, 123
IRS on, 79
taxes and taxation, 29
after-tax cash flow, 72
cash flow before, 70
counsel, 122
deductions, 73–74
depreciation allowance and, 73
federal tax table, 76
NNN lease and, 256–257
pre-tax cash flow, 72
1040 tax return, 120–121
Tax Reform Act of 1986, 73
team building, 194
considerations in, 46
steps, 48–49
1040 tax return, 120–121
tenant improvements (TIs), 232, 285
tenant's responsibilities, in property management, 156–157
termite inspection, 136–137
TFTs. *See* transactions fell through
thank-you notes, 85, 138
time blocking, for residential real estate agents, 6
TIs (tenant improvements), 232, 285
title insurance, 27

320 *Index*

transactions fell through (TFTs),
46
trust, listing proposal book
and, 107
trust agreement, 132–133
trust fund handling of
customer deposits, 266
Tucson, 242
type A personalities, 107

United States
escrow in, 130
MLS in, 116
unlawful detainer actions,
159–160
USA Today, 113

vacancy rates, 66–67, 69–70,
214
vacations, 93

verbal listing, 103–104
Victorian apartment-houses, 35
Vosburgh, Maureen, 181

Walgreens, 241
Wall Street Journal, 113
Wal-Mart, 241
waterbeds, in commercial leases,
167
WCR (Women's Council of
REALTORS®), 79
weekend work, 17–18
weighted cost per square
foot, 65
willful nondisclosure, 270
Women's Council of
REALTORS® (WCR), 79
wood-frame construction, 250

year-end assessment, 97